HAMILTON'S GUIDE

YELLOWSTONE
National Park

by
ALAN W. CUNDALL

and
HERBERT T. LYSTRUP
FORMER RANGER NATURALIST

Published & Distributed by
Hamilton Stores Inc., P.O. Box 250, West Yellowstone, Montana 59758

"...what God hath wrought"

FRONT COVER
PHOTOS CLOCKWISE:

Grand Canyon of the Yellowstone,
Old Faithful, Tower Fall,
West Thumb on Yellowstone Lake,
North Entrance Archway,
Indian Paintbrush

BACK COVER
SPRING: Bison and Calf
SUMMER: Yellowstone River
FALL: Elk
WINTER: Lower Falls &
        Grand Canyon of
        Yellowstone in Winter

Pages 2, 3
Lower Falls of the Yellowstone
& Grand Canyon in Summer & Winter

DESIGNED BY LEE TERMINELLO

LMPC INTERNATIONAL • Printed in Hong Kong

CONTENTS

Firehole River

Blue Gentian, Official Flower of Yellowstone National Park

FOREWORD

This is a revised, and updated version of the popular **Hamilton's Guide to Yellowstone National Park.** I think you'll find, as I did, that it is an exceptionally well-written presentation of the great natural features of our Park in all their beauty and grandeur; and contains useful information about the National Park Service which protects this vast public domain.

Herb Lystrup's 37 years of service as a Seasonal Park Ranger Naturalist at Yellowstone, and his long experience as an educator, qualified him to present the historical and scientific facts as perhaps no other person could. We are indebted, as well, to travel writer Alan Cundall for his enthusiastic and very thorough description of the popular trip around the Grand Loop Road, each step described in terms which have a special appeal to both newcomers and repeat visitors.

It's unfortunate, but too many visitors today make a hurried tour of the southern section of the Loop for a view of the Canyon and the geyser basins; or grab just a glimpse of Old Faithful and the nearby thermal features—and leave. Too many fail to enjoy the scenic northern half of the Park. All too few come with sufficient budgeted time and proper equipment for a wilderness experience in the magnificent, uncrowded back country. Seldom will the performance of Yellowstone's wonders coincide with your arrival. Experienced visitors learn to settle down and wait. They are never disappointed. Yellowstone Park has the most exciting hot-spring activity in the United States; the largest and most primitive wild regions, exclusive of Alaska. This guidebook with its fold-out map does not overlook any of these—and it is my fondest hope you will not either!

This definitive guidebook also recognizes the importance of the work of our dedicated Park Rangers and Ranger Naturalists and goes a long way toward making their work easier. Our rangers have been trained to make your stay more enjoyable and meaningful through interpretation of the natural features of the Park—by exhibits at museums and visitor centers, evening campfire talks, walks along specially-built nature trails, all-day hikes, and by seeing that free literature and historical markers are available where they will be most helpful.

As one who has known the 3,472 square miles of Yellowstone Park for over half a century, I heartily recommend this excellent guidebook. It will vastly increase your knowledge and enjoyment of your trip, and it may well be a cherished memory item in your library until such time as you can come back to stay with us again.

HORACE M. ALBRIGHT
*Former Superintendent of Yellowstone National Park
and Former Director of the National Park Service*

WELCOME TO

YELLOWSTONE NATIONAL PARK

Welcome to Yellowstone Park, the world's first National Park. Known today as "the grand old park," it was set aside by the Act of Dedication which was approved by Congress and signed by President Ulysses S. Grant on March 1, 1872.

A few extracts from the Act seem pertinent. The Park was

> ". . . set apart as a public park or pleasuring ground for the benefit and enjoyment of the people. The said public park shall be under the exclusive control of the Secretary of the Interior, whose duty it shall be, as soon as practicable, to make and publish such rules and regulations as he may deem proper for the care and management of the same. Such regulations shall provide for the preservation from injury or spoliation of all timber, mineral deposits, natural curiosities, or wonders within said park, and their retention in their natural conditions."

Today, in our generation, it becomes our duty to keep the natural phenomena in perpetuity for all mankind for all time. One of the mottoes of the Park Service is, "For the benefit and enjoyment of the people." We owe a tremendous debt of gratitude for the vision and foresight of those who made it possible for us to "benefit and enjoy" the wonders of Yellowstone. Let it not be said of our generation that we were delinquent in our duty. Let us keep inviolate for our children and their children "what God hath wrought."

Yellowstone is the greatest wildlife sanctuary in the United States. Everyone is welcome to share the natural phenomena so generously lavished over mountains, meadows, forests, streams, and lakes. It is *here,* not in any artificial manifestation, but in pristine loveliness to be enjoyed by all.

Welcome to Yellowstone National Park!

Next pages 10, 11: The Storm and the Sun on Old Faithful Geyser ►

THE GRAND LOOP ROAD

—A MILE-BY-MILE DESCRIPTION
OF YOUR TRIP AROUND THE PARK

The major section of this guidebook is a description of the 300 miles of roads within Yellowstone Park. Before starting your trip, consult the fold-out map in the back of the book. You'll note that the main highway, called the Grand Loop, forms a lopsided "figure 8" in the center of the Park and takes you to the most popular areas. The Grand Loop Road covers a distance of 142 miles and may be traveled clockwise or counter-clockwise. It carries two-way traffic and the speed limit is 45 mph unless otherwise posted.

There are five entrance roads leading into the Park and they all feed into the Grand Loop. (A sixth entrance, the Bechler Entrance, is accessible only from Ashton, Idaho. It dead-ends at a campground and does not meet the Grand Loop Road.) The center of the Grand Loop Road is bisected by a two-way road connecting Norris Junction and Canyon Junction, a distance of 12 miles.

The text of this section of the book begins at the West Entrance which is practically in the "suburbs" of West Yellowstone, Montana. The text and pictures will take you along the West Entrance Road to the Grand Loop, then south to follow the Loop around the Park, counter-clockwise. The various other entrance roads and connecting roads are described as you come across them in your "journey," starting from where each enters the Park and tracing each back to the Loop.

Obviously, if you enter the Park from other than the West Entrance, you will want to start reading at that point in the text and work your way back to the beginning. The Table of Contents in the front, giving the page numbers for the five entrances, and the map in the back, will help you find your place in the book (and in the Park).

There are numerous directional signs and historical attraction markers. Also, if you tune your car radio to 1610 on the AM dial whenever you see one of the many "Tune 1610" roadside signs, you will hear recorded safety messages and general park information.

The most important thing to remember is to take the time to really understand and appreciate what you are seeing. Yellowstone Park is yours to enjoy. Drive at a leisurely pace and stop at the many pull-out parking places and vista points. (This will not only enable you to enjoy the Park as fully as possible, but it will also allow the cars behind you—who may have already seen this portion of the Park—to pass.) Walk the trails, read the historical markers, visit the ranger exhibits, wonder at the sights, and marvel at the sounds. You'll discover, as have millions before you, that there is no place on earth like Yellowstone National Park.

The GRAND LOOP
(See inside back cover for complete map.)

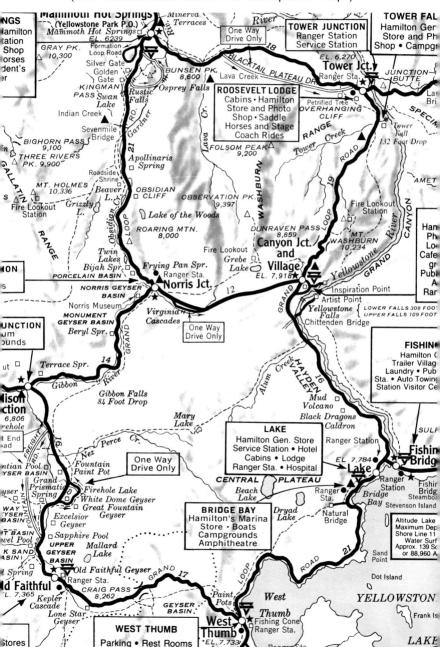

NGS
Hamilton
station
Shop
orses
dent's
er

Mammoth Hot Springs
(Yellowstone Park P.O.)
Mammoth Hot Springs
EL. 6239

TOWER JUNCTION
Ranger Station
Service Station
EL. 6,270

TOWER FAL
Hamilton Ger
Store and Ph
Shop • Campg

Minerva
Terraces

River

One Way
Drive Only

Tower Jct.
Ranger Sta.

JUNCTION
BUTTE

GRAY PK.
10,300

Formation
Loop Road

18

BLACKTAIL PLATEAU DR

La
Bri

Silver Gate
Golden
Gate

BUNSEN PK.
8,600

Lava Creek

SPECIA

KINGMAN
PASS

Osprey Falls

Rustic
Falls

ROOSEVELT LODGE
Cabins • Hamilton
Store and Photo
Shop • Saddle
Horses and Stage
Coach Rides

Petrified Tree
OVERHANGING
CLIFF

Tower
Fall
132 Foot Drop

AMET

Swan
Lake

Indian Creek

BIGHORN PASS
9,100

Sevenmile
Bridge

THREE RIVERS
PK. 9,900

Apollinaris
Spring

FOLSOM PEAK
9,200

Tower Creek

RANGE

ROAD

Han
Ph
Lo
Cafe
gr
Pub
A
Rar

GALLATIN

Roadside
Shrine

MT. HOLMES
10,336

Beaver
L.

OBSIDIAN
CLIFF

OBSERVATION PK.
9,397

WASHBURN

Fire Lookout
Station

Fire Lookout
Station

Grizzly
L.

Lake of the Woods

19

ION
s

ROARING MTN.
8,000

DUNRAVEN PASS
8,859

MT.
WASHBURN
10,234

LOOP

GRAND

River

CANYON

RANGE

Twin
Lakes
Bijah Spr.

Fire Lookout

**Canyon Jct.
and
Village**
EL. 7,918

Grebe
Lake

Yellowstone

PORCELAIN BASIN

Frying Pan Spr.
Ranger Sta.

Inspiration Point

UNCTION
um
ounds

**NORRIS GEYSER
BASIN**

Norris Jct.

12

Artist Point

Yellowstone
Falls

LOWER FALLS 308 FOO
UPPER FALLS 109 FOOT

Norris Museum

**MONUMENT
GEYSER BASIN**
Beryl Spr.

Virginia
Cascades

Chittenden Bridge

One Way
Drive Only

FISHIN
Hamilton
Trailer Villag
Laundry • Pub
Sta. • Auto Towing
Station Visitor Ce

14

Terrace Spr.

Gibbon

River

GRAND

ison
ction
6,806
ehole

Gibbon Falls
84 Foot Drop

Mary
Lake

HAYDEN

Alum Creek

VALLEY

16

Mud
Volcano

Black Dragons
Caldron

SULF

l End
ad

16

Perce

Nez
Fountain
Paint Pot

Cr.

One Way
Drive Only

LAKE
Hamilton Gen. Store
Service Station • Hotel
Cabins • Lodge
Ranger Sta. • Hospital

Ranger Station

EL. 7,784

Fishin
Bridg

FISHING

ntian
YSER BASIN

Grand
Prismatic
Spring

Firehole Lake
White Dome Geyser
Great Fountain
Geyser

CENTRAL

PLATEAU

Beach
Lake

Lake

Ranger
Station

Fishi
Brid
Steamboa

ser

Stevenson Island

WAY
BASIN

Excelsior
Geyser

Ranger
Sta.

Bridge
Bay

BASIN
vel Pool

Sapphire Pool
Mallard
Lake

BRIDGE BAY
Hamilton's Marina
Store • Boats
Campgrounds
Amphitheatre

Dryad
Lake

Natural
Bridge

Altitude Lake
Maximum Dep
Shore Line 11
Water Surf
Approx. 139 Sc
or 88,960 A

K SAND
ASIN

**UPPER
GEYSER
BASIN**

l Spring

GRAND

17

Sand
Point

d Faithful
L. 7,365

Old Faithful Geyser
Ranger Sta.

LOOP

ROAD

Dot Island

Kepler
Cascade

CRAIG PASS
8,262

Lone Star
Geyser

Paint
Pots

West
Thumb

YELLOWSTON

WEST THUMB
Parking • Rest Rooms
Boardwalk

tores
Hotel

**West
Thumb**
EL. 7,733

GEYSER
BASIN

Fishing Cone
Ranger Sta.

Frank Is

Ranger Sta.

LAKE

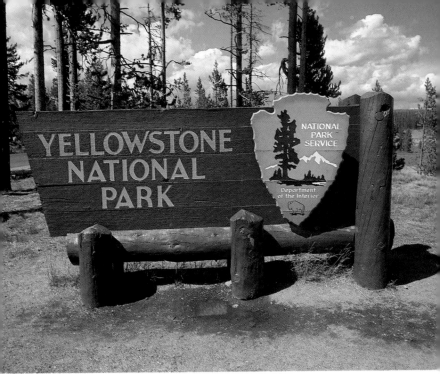

Yellowstone Entrance Sign

WEST ENTRANCE TO MADISON JUNCTION

From the West Entrance (and the town of West Yellowstone, Montana) to Madison Junction is a 14-mile trip along the **Madison River** through canyons and open meadows. The Madison River is flowing toward you and goes out of the Park to be joined by the Gallatin and Jefferson Rivers which form the Missouri River near Three Forks, Montana.

The Madison River, one of the world's famous trout fishing streams, was named by the Lewis and Clark Expedition in honor of James Madison, then Secretary of State under Thomas Jefferson and later President.

West Yellowstone, Montana, is a thriving, friendly town with close ties to the Park. It has numerous motels and trailer sites as well as other resort facilities such as campgrounds, service stations, grocery stores, medical facilites, Park bus transportation, etc. Some thirty miles distant is the area of the Madison Canyon (Hebgen Lake) Earthquake of 1959. The U.S. Forest service operates a visitor center there and forest rangers conduct "on-the-spot" presentations to tell the story of the Earthquake.

Just before the West Gate Entrance to your right is a short side road that leads to the Hamilton Stores, Inc. general offices and warehouse. Hamilton Stores, Inc. operates general stores, marina store, and photo shops within Yellowstone Park and offers a wide selection of fine gifts, souvenirs, photo supplies, groceries, fishing/camping equipment, Indian artwork, clothing and food service.

The **Madison Canyon Road** from West Yellowstone, Montana, to Madison Junction was a logical, natural entrance to the Park long before Yellowstone was created as a National Park. The early trappers simply followed the Madison River upstream to its confluence with the Gibbon and Firehole Rivers. The various stagecoaches and carriages used the same course when primitive roads were constructed. When automobiles were permitted to enter Yellowstone in 1915, the road was improved again. However, the dirt roads were frequently dusty, muddy, and bumpy. Improvement continued with new bridges, straightened curves, and a two-lane highway; and the road is still being improved today.

The Madison Canyon Road is also geologically significant. Evidence of the 1959 earthquake and its subsequent tremors can be seen in and on both sides of the river as you travel along the road. Look at the huge boulders in the river. Those which are not as weatherworn (darkly shaded) or as fully covered with lichen as the older rocks were jolted loose in 1959. The older rocks probably crashed into the river as a result of earlier earthquake tremors.

Rock slides are clearly visible on the forested mountain slopes where bounding rocks cut a swath through the trees—breaking, mashing, and scattering them in helter-skelter fashion.

Trumpeter Swans

As you travel about two miles into the Madison River Valley, note the cliffs that rise 700 feet to the Madison Plateau. Several of the Park's major hydrothermal features are found along the edge of this plateau. These cliffs are formed mostly of rhyolite (as is much of the rock and soil throughout the Park) which was spewed forth in a giant volcanic eruption.

About seven miles from the West Entrance, you will cross the Madison River into a wide canyon. The rhyolite walls and floor of this canyon were originally pink or grey, but they have weathered black and are now being worked upon by brightly-colored lichens. Eventually, the lichen will break down the rocks and turn them into soil.

Elk can often be seen grazing in the meadows and along the fringes of the forests. You may catch a glimpse of mule deer (black tail deer) as they scamper deeper into the forest. Along the river, watch for Canada Geese, Great Blue Herons, and a wide variety of ducks. In the area of **Seven Mile Bridge,** rare trumpeter swans find the river to their liking. They nest in Yellowstone and in a very few other places in North America. Their deep trumpet-like cry can be heard two miles away.

The West Entrance Road passes between **Mount Haynes** and **Mount Jackson,** both are over 8,200 feet high. They were named for early Yellowstone pioneer photographers. Look westward and you'll see ragged peaks in Wyoming, Montana and Idaho—a three-state panorama.

Where the West Entrance Road meets the **Grand Loop,** the Madison River ends—or, rather, *begins*—since this is where the Firehole and Gibbon Rivers come together to form the Madison. Facilities at **Madison Junction** include a campground, amphitheater, ranger station, and Explorer's Museum. However, there are no lodging facilities, stores, or service stations. The Explorer's Museum features exhibits of early explorations and explains how Yellowstone came to be set aside as the world's first National Park.

If you can, walk the short distance out behind the Museum, and look across to where the Firehole River, emerging from Firehole Canyon, converges with the Gibbon River to form the Madison. It was here that the 19 members of the Washburn-Langford-Doane expedition of 1870 spent the last night of their expedition. Reportedly, they sat around a campfire discussing the wonders they had seen and the talk turned to what should be done with the area. It was suggested that claims be staked on the most scenic regions. But a more altruistic idea caught everyone's imagination—that the entire area be set aside as a National park for the benefit and enjoyment of all people. When they returned home, the expedition members convinced others of the importance of the idea, and worked unstintingly for legislation to make the dream a reality.

MADISON JUNCTION TO OLD FAITHFUL

Driving south on the Grand Loop (headed toward Old Faithful), **National Park Mountain** is on your right. It is not a "true" mountain, but an extension of the Madison Plateau.

Just beyond where the road crosses the river, there is an interesting two-mile side trip on the **Firehole Canyon Road** (one-way south). Once an Indian trail, it takes you through the deep Firehole Canyon with its 800-foot black walls (formed by lava flows) to view **Firehole Falls** and the **Firehole Cascades.**

Firehole Falls has a 40-foot drop into a rocky glen. It then dashes into a stretch of white, churning water—the exciting Firehole Cascades.

You'll rejoin the main road and continue southward across Nez Perce Creek, named for Chief Joseph's band of Nez Perce Indians who, as they were fleeing from the Army, passed this spot. Bison (Buffalo) often graze in the wildflower-filled meadows along the creek. The deep blue flowers with the erect tubular petals are Rocky Mountain Fringed Gentians, the official Yellowstone Park flower.

Fountain Flats Drive is an old, two-way freight road that runs behind Lower and Midway Geyser Basins. While it is another interesting side trip off the main road, it dead-ends for auto traffic after three miles and continues as a bicycle and foot trail to rejoin the Grand Loop. In winter, it is a one-way snowmobile road and cross-country ski trail. The **Imperial Geyser** and **Fairy Falls** can be reached from trails along this road.

If you stay on the Grand Loop, just south of the turn-off to the freight road you'll come to the large parking area for the **Fountain Paint Pots.** In one half-mile walk—safely guided on the wooden paths—you'll see **Silex Spring, Morning Geyser, Fountain Geyser, Jet Geyser, Spasm Geyser, Jelly Geyser, Clepsydra Geyser,** the bubbling **Fountain Paint Pots,** and far out on the basin—**Kaleidoscope Geyser,** erupting to heights of 30 to 50 feet.

The **Fountain Paint Pots** are an intriguing phenomena. Visitors are fascinated watching the mud bubbles boil, gurgle, growl, and burst to fling the mud about in stringy lumps. The mud is composed of clay and silica which were formed by chemical decomposition of rock minerals. The underlying rocks are largely rhyolite (containing silica and feldspar) which, with acid waters, breaks down to hydrous aluminum silicates in the form of clay. The water beneath the surface is held in glacial gravels and is heated by superheated gases rising from magmatic source. The colorings, due to the various minerals, are in shades of pink, orange, and pale blue. Seasonally, depending upon the water supply, the Paint Pots change from a diluted, runny goop to a heavy, viscous mud.

The run-off water channel from Clepsydra, Spasm, and Jelly Geysers support the algae in a color display as brilliant as any in the Park.

Firehole River, Upper Geyser Basin

Firehole Falls, Firehole Canyon

Grotto Geyser, Upper Geyser Basin

Grand Prismatic Spring

The upright dead Lodgepole Pines with the white bases (near **Celestine Pool**) were at one time standing in water. When the water changed course, they were "drowned." The upper parts became encrusted with silicon dioxide. The bases of the trees have become preserved by the capillary action of the water, laden with silica, which filled the cell spaces. The tree dies, but the woody walls remained. Trees of this type are common on many geyser basins and some have been standing this way since long before the Park was discovered. (The Park Rangers facetiously call these the "Dead Dog Forests." Why? Because the trees have no "bark," of course!)

Firehole Lake Drive is a one-way side road that, again, was constructed to show you a special area of interest and then put you back on the main road. Firehole Lake Drive is three miles not to be missed!

The geysers you'll encounter first on the loop are **White Dome, Pine Cone, Narcissus, Steady,** and **Firehole Lake** (Hot Lake) itself, one of the Park's largest hot pools.

The vents in Firehole Lake release large bubbles of gas. These bubbles expand as they encounter less pressure reaching the surface and light from the sky, reflected through them, appears as a "bunsen blue flame."

Great Fountain Geyser is a typical fountain-type geyser. When it is quiet between eruptions (or "play"), it is much like a hot spring with water low in its crater. When an eruption is imminent, the bowl of the crater fills and overflows its ledge, apparently flushing out cooler, near-surface water. There follows a visible lifting of the body of water with increased overflow. Suddenly, a great fan-like jets break free and the geyser erupts dramatically with a series of great bursts separated by brief pauses. Maximum height is usually 100 to 150 feet, but rare bursts have reached 230 feet. The eruption may last up to 75 minutes; 50 to 60 minutes is more usual. The interval between eruptions is seven to fifteen hours, so you're lucky if the Great Fountain performs when you are in the audience.

Nearby **White Dome Geyser,** a tall, cone-type geyser, is conspicuous over the entire basin. It erupts for 2 minutes, blowing hot water through the opening at its top to heights varying up to 30 feet.

Geysers are a lot like people. Some are fairly predictable, while others are cantankerous and quite unpredictable. No two are alike, but all are fascinating to watch, whether they're large or small. Geysers are forms of hot springs which intermittently eject water several inches or several hundred feet. (Sponge Geyser in the Upper Geyser Basin is an example of a very small geyser.)

The major features of **Midway Geyser Basin** enroute to Old Faithful are reached from the parking area by walking across the bridge spanning the Firehole River. The scalding hot water which pours into the river from **Excelsior Geyser** flows at the rate of six cubic feet per second. That's over five million gallons of 199-degree water a day for 1½ billion gallons a year! Excelsior Geyser erupted on September 14, 1985 to the height of 55 feet and lasted 46 hours. The last known prior eruption was in 1888.

Grand Prismatic Spring is 370 feet in diameter and the largest of Yellowstone's hot springs. It is surely one of the most beautiful! The deep water in the center is an intense azure blue. At the edges, the hot water temperature is ideal for algae to grow, producing colors ranging from orange and green to golden brown. The water spilling over ripple-like miniature terraces supports algae of various pastel shades. At first, the hot vapors rising over Grand Prismatic Spring appear to be colored. Actually, the algae below reflect their colors through the hot vapors.

For a breathtaking view of **Midway Basin,** hike the short distance across the parking area up the north slope to Bluff Point. The panorama before you is something from another world. Here is an opportunity for you to photograph Grand Prismatic Spring, Excelsior Geyser Crater, Indigo Spring, Turquoise Pool, Firehole River, and Twin Buttes, all on one exposure. You almost *have* to take a picture of it because your friends back home won't believe it.

Continuing south past Rabbit Creek and the Mallard Creek picnic area, a short side road leads to the **Biscuit Basin** parking area. Next, cross the foot bridge to **Sapphire Pool** which, before the 1959 earthquake, was a geyser which erupted to heights of 10 or 12 feet. A bridge-like walk skirted a portion of the hot water crater from which it was possible to observe clusters of large gaseous bubbles, deep in blue hot water, rising and becoming larger as they moved to the surface to break violently into eruption. Around the edges of the crater were biscuit-like geyserite mounds which gave Biscuit Basin its homespun name. The earthquake disrupted the usual activity with violent eruptions, reaching heights of 100 feet and scattering the huge geyserite biscuits far out on the basin. Now Sapphire no longer erupts.

Nearby is **Jewel Geyser** which erupts about every 12 to 15 minutes to heights up to 22 feet. On the ledge surrounding the orifice are tiny, pearl-like, solid geyserite balls set in colorful algae. Balls such as these are formed around a grain of sand, or similar substance, which serves as a nucleus around which the siliceous material is deposited. Jewel Geyser is very photogenic. Stand on the boardwalk at a spot where the entire water column can be included, and you can capture even the water droplets in the spray. Since the interval of eruptions is short, watch one eruption before you take a picture so you won't be doused by the spray.

Other features to observe along the walk include **Shell Geyser, Silver Globe, Avoca Spring,** and **Mustard Spring.** Note the yellow flowers, Mimu-

*Sunset at White
Dome Geyser,
Lower
Geyser Basin*

Thumb Paint Pots

Firehole River

Cliff Geyser in Black Sand Basin

lus or Monkeyflower, growing along the edges of hot water springs and run-off channels.

At the west end of Biscuit Basin, near Avoca Spring (which frequently performs as a geyser), a side trail leads to **Mystic Falls.** This gently rolling trail meanders along the Little Firehole River 0.8 miles through a mature forest alive with wildflowers, chipmunks, and birds. Occasionally, a marmot may be seen on the open rock slopes. Near the end of the trail, you'll discover several beautiful cascades. A climb up several short switchbacks to an overlook will reward you with an impressive view of the 70-foot drop of Mystic Falls with its billowing spray of steaming hot springs.

The Grand Loop Road continues southward another two miles toward **Black Sand Basin** and some of the most beautiful thermal scenery in the Park. Observe the hot springs on the flanks of the mountain to the right, displayed in reds and oranges similar to tomato soup. The early stagecoach drivers referred to the springs as "Tomato Soup Springs," but they are formally named **Hillside Springs.**

After the road leaves the forest, you'll see steam rising from **Black Sand Pool** and its broad, white sinter outwash on the left. Ahead to the right is the parking lot at Black Sand Basin. If you'll examine the coarse, black grains of obsidian sand at the road-cuts and along the margins of the parking area, you'll see why this thermal basin got its name.

Ahead of you is a dazzling color display. The hot springs and geysers are divided by the cold waters of **Iron Creek,** while the hot water run-off channels provide an environment for various species of algae.

On the nearside of the creek, **Opalescent Pool** with its milky blue tint is filled by the almost continuous splashing and discharge of **Spouter Geyser.**

Cliff Geyser on the opposite creek bank is interesting because it is so near to the creek. It is a geyser that varies from year-to-year. When it erupts, the duration may vary from 10 minutes to 2 to 3 hours, and it may burst as high as 50 feet in the air.

The boardwalk leads you past many small bubbling vents, **Green Spring,** and onto the footbridge across Iron Creek. Here in the center of Black Sand Basin, the trail divides. To the right is **Rainbow Pool,** a large hot spring with an intensely blue center. The overflowing water spills out on the surrounding basin and cools sufficiently to permit the growth of yellow, orange, brown, and green algae in an artist's palette of color. Nearby Sunset Lake vies with Rainbow Pool for beauty and color iridescence.

Near Rainbow Pool was once the location of **Handkerchief Pool,** severly damaged by vandals in the late Twenties. (It is contrary to Federal regulations to tamper with any of the thermal features in Yellowstone.)

Retrace your steps to the boardwalk junction and continue ahead to **Emerald Pool.** The combination of blue sky, yellow algae, and the depth of the thermal pool produces the beautiful green which makes Emerald Pool an often-photographed favorite of visitors.

The tiny blue flowers conspicuous along the boardwalk are members of the Iris family named Blue-eyed Grass. Poison Hemlock (also called Water Hemlock), a member of the carrot family, is the tall plant with large, finely-cut leaves and white flowers in umbels. It grows in moist soil such as that found near Iron Creek.

After returning to the Grand Loop Road, turn right and you will immediately enter a short section of divided highway. To reach **Old Faithful Geyser** and the **Upper Geyser Basin,** keep to the right up the entrance ramp onto the overpass. Please use extreme caution as there are areas of two-way traffic. Be alert to yield the right of way when merging.

Signs will direct you to Old Faithful (you can hardly miss it!) where facilities include Hamilton General Stores, Photo Shop, the turn-of-the-century Old Faithful Inn, Old Faithful Lodge, cabins, cafeteria, post office, service stations, visitor center, ranger station and showers at the Old Faithful Lodge.

As with each major stop, you may want to check at the visitor center. Here, a free movie describing the different types of thermal features is shown frequently; and special exhibits, displays on weather, earthquake activity, and other selected topics are presented. Check with the Park Ranger Naturalist at the Information Desk on what special programs are scheduled for the Old Faithful area. There are almost always guided walks, self-guiding trails, all-day hikes, and evening programs.

Castle Geyser

Spouter Geyser, Black Sand Basin

Iron Creek, Black Sand Basin

Riverside Geyser, Upper Geyser Basin

Emerald Pool at Black Sand Basin

Old Faithful is the world's best-known geyser and one of the most publicized natural phenomenon of any sort. As most first-time visitors do not realize, it is neither the largest, highest, nor most regular geyser in the Park—but it *is* consistent. Its heights, intervals, and lengths of eruption have varied very little in the over 100 years since it was found and named by the Washburn Party in 1870.

Old Faithful does not erupt every hour on the hour, but it does erupt 18 to 21 times every day, which is what gave it its "hourly" reputation. Unlike most geysers, it has two patterns of eruption—short ones that last 1½ to 2 minutes and long ones that last 3 to 5 minutes.

Several surges of water over the rim of the crater are the first signs that the column of water is about to rise. The column normally reaches maximum height in 15 to 20 seconds. The maximum height averages 130 feet, but has gone as high as 184 feet. (The stronger the wind, the lower the height of the eruption is apt to be; the wind blows the top off the ascending column of water and thus reduces the height of play.) After about 20 seconds of play, the water column lowers rapidly and the eruption ends with a few last-gasps of steam. Old Faithful discharges up to 7,500 gallons of water per eruption.

With the right wind conditions and the right lighting, it is an amazing sight to behold—one worthy of the world's most famous geyser.

Check at the visitor center for the approximate time of the next eruption

Various Faces of Old Faithful

of Old Faithful and the other major geysers nearby. This time is estimated by the Park rangers by measuring the duration of an eruption, using a stopwatch. They then refer to a formula designed by Dr. George D. Marler, author of several texts on Old Faithful and other geysers in the area. Briefly, the formula proves that the longer the eruption, the longer the interval before the next display. And vice versa.

As awesome a sight as Old Faithful is, too many "busy" visitors simply do not allow enough time to see everything the Upper Geyser Basin and the Park have to offer. They drive directly to the area, take a picture of one eruption of Old Faithful, and go home and boast to their friends that they "really saw Yellowstone." You should plan to spend at least several hours to appreciate the Old Faithful area and a stay of several days is even more rewarding. It is the Upper Geyser Basin that constitutes the whole phenomenon, not just its faithful star performer; and, of course, it is the total Park which is the true attraction.

Walking north from the entrance of Hamilton's Lower General Store which is north of Old Faithful Inn, the first geyser you come to is **Castle Geyser** which has a huge cone (120 feet around) and looks like the ruins of an old castle tower. A typical cone type geyser with its orifice at the top, it erupts hot water to heights from 60 to 100 feet.

Pages 30, 31: Old Faithful Geyser ▶

Morning Glory Pool

Grand Geyser, along the trail, deserves its name. It is a typical fountain-type geyser. Seeing Grand Geyser's first burst is an unforgettable experience. The large crater fills with hot water which bulges and splashes over the ledge. Suddenly, without warning, a mass of water breaks free to form a widening fan, from which sky-flung plumes rocket to heights of 200 feet, each trying to out-do the others. These eruptions, one after another, may continue from 15 to 45 minutes. The last spurts may be as high or higher than the first!

From Grand Geyser, walks are constructed to **Sawmill, Tardy,** and **Castle** geysers. To the north, you'll encounter the Daisy Geyser group including the erratic **Daisy** and **Splendid Geysers, Punch Bowl Spring,** and **Black Sand Pool.**

Grotto Geyser, with its peculiar cone, is interesting even when not erupting. About half the time, it is in a splashy, steamy, eruptive phase, but rarely gets more than 12 feet high. Other geysers in this area include: **Spa, Rocket, Surprise, Giant Mastiff, Bijou,** and **Oblong.**

Riverside Geyser is across the river to the right, actually located on the river bank. Although its intervals are long (6 to 8½ hours), Riverside Geyser is more regular than Old Faithful. It erupts for 20 minutes to heights nearing 80 feet at an angle over the river. Because of its duration, you easily can take several pictures from different angles during one eruption.

A little further on to the left is **Morning Glory Pool,** considered by many to be one of the most beautiful of the hot springs. It was disturbed by the 1959 earthquake to such an extent that its water became cloudy. In recent years, however, it has cleared up and again reflects the blue of the sky. Its morning glory shape reflects the deepest blue when the sun is highest in the sky.

From the guard rail along the trail to the left, observe **Artemisia Geyser.** Look down on the formations surrounding the geyser and note the intricate designs of geyserite around the many collecting pools. The maze of tiny terraces is the result of geyserite deposition. The gray-green color may have suggested the name Artemisia, which is the generic name of sagebrush. Artemisia erupts about once a day for approximately 15 minutes and reaches a height of 35 feet.

Follow the constructed trail around Old Faithful Geyser across the Firehole River to **Geyser Hill.** The Firehole River receives the run-off water from many hot springs and geysers, and by the time the Midway Geyser Basin is passed, its temperature is increased as much as 30 degrees. Surprisingly, the water supports fish and other wildlife. **Plume Geyser,** which erupts at intervals of 30 to 50 minutes to heights of 25 feet, is a relative newcomer. It first became active in 1942, and exposed its center vent during the spring of 1973.

Beehive Geyser, whose cone is said to resemble a beehive, is a major geyser erupting to a height of 150 to 180 feet. A noisy display once or twice a day, and it often has long inactive periods. **Giantess Geyser** is a large fountain geyser which erupts very rarely. However, when the Giantess does erupt, the area shakes with underground explosions, water is hurled 100 to 200 feet into the air, and eruptions continue intermittently for 12 to 43 hours!

Other features to see on Geyser Hill include **Vault Geyser, Teakettle Spring, Pump Geyser, Sponge Geyser** (which erupts a few inches about every 45 seconds), **Beach Spring, Ear Spring,** and the **Lion Geyser Group** (Lion, Lioness, Big Cub, and Little Cub).

A foot trail leads to **Observation Point** where you'll be rewarded with a magnificent view of the Upper Geyser Basin and Old Faithful. Time your walk to coincide with an eruption of Old Faithful for a startling view. Note how the people are drawn as if by a magnet as they approach the log seats and rim the area on the boardwalks far below. A photograph looking down on Old Faithful will probably be the one you will most treasure.

Along the Observation Point trail near the rocky top, watch for the tiny pika (also called conies), distant cousins of the rabbit. Farther down the trail, you are almost certain to see and hear yellowbelly marmots where they lie on the large rocks to absorb warmth from the sun. You can't miss their shrill, distinctive whistle. The marmots are also referred to as woodchucks or whistle pigs. They are true hibernators. Red squirrels are common in the pine forests, and you'll hear them chattering as they gather pine cones.

A part of the trail on the return from Observation Point continues to **Solitary Geyser.** The dwarf huckleberry on either side of the trail is a member of the blueberry family, and produces a sweet berry which is much relished by black bears. The mint bed near water seepage announces itself with its distinctive mint odor. Wild strawberries, smaller but just as tasty as the domestic varieties, are also common in this part of the Park.

Solitary Geyser erupts for about 2 minutes at intervals of 2 to 6 minutes to heights of 25 feet. Notice the beautiful colors made by the algae in the hot water channels.

Near **Beach Spring,** look for the yellow columbine and wild onion with several species showing colors of red, purple, and white. The constructed trail takes you over Geyser Hill to the Old Faithful Visitor Center.

West Thumb Geyser Basin

OLD FAITHFUL TO WEST THUMB

Continuing approximately 1½ miles on the Grand Loop Road towards **West Thumb Junction,** you'll come to the **Kepler Cascades** parking area. Walk just a few steps to the wooden platform for a splendid view of a series of falls and cascades tumbling over a hundred feet between sheer canyon walls. You may be fortunate enough to catch a glimpse of the water ouzel or dipper, a short, stubby, clownish bird of dark gray color. They feed on aquatic larvae and even walk under water on the bottoms of streams.

Beyond Kepler Cascades is a 2½ mile trail to **Lone Star Geyser** which erupts from a 12-foot cone to heights of 35 feet. The main eruption is preceded by several short eruptions for several minutes. These subside and the main eruption occurs 15 to 20 minutes later with a three-hour interval between eruptions. The geyser cone is impressive even without an eruption.

Up stream from Lone Star Geyser, a marked foot trail over a bridge leads 7½ miles to **Shoshone Geyser Basin.** This makes a pleasant one-day hike.

Continuing east on the Grand Loop Road, be sure and stop at **Isa Lake** on Craig Pass (8,261 feet). Tiny, gem-like Isa Lake actually straddles the Continental Divide and its water flows in one direction to the Atlantic Ocean

◀ *Previous pages 34, 35: Old Faithful Geyser, Grand Geyser, Castle Geyser*

and in the other to the Pacific Ocean. The water flowing west reaches the Firehole River, the Madison, Missouri, Mississippi, Gulf of Mexico, and—finally—the Atlantic Ocean. The flow from Isa Lake to the east reaches Herron Creek, De Lacy Creek, Shoshone Lake, Lewis Lake, Lewis River, Snake River, Columbia River, and—at last!—the Pacific Ocean.

Isa Lake is covered in midsummer with golden water lillies with large yellow flowers and leaves from 4 to 12 inches long. This plant is also called Wokas and is most beautiful in August.

A foot trail at De Lacy Creek reaches **Shoshone Lake** after a three-mile walk. Often, moose may be seen feeding on plants in the swampy bottom lands of the creek.

Back on the Grand Loop Road continuing east, **Shoshone Point** on clear days affords a remarkable view of the Teton Mountain Range thirty miles distant in Grand Teton National Park. Shoshone Lake, surrounded by dense forests, typifies a true wilderness area.

Once again, you'll cross the **Continental Divide.** This time, the elevation is 8,391 feet. You'll be able to see huge Yellowstone Lake for the first time as it expansively spreads to the mountains far to the east. You'll be surrounded on both sides of the road with an almost impenetrable forest of pines. This forest is left purposely in its natural state in keeping with National Park policy. The dead and fallen trees will decompose and return to the soil to enrich it for future growth. This same practice is observed when a wild animal dies in the forest. The body is left as carrion for the other animals; the skeleton eventually becomes a part of the soil, too.

Duck Lake to the left below the road is a clear jewel in a forest of green. This little lake is the supply of drinking water for West Thumb. (Sorry, no fishing.)

West Thumb Junction is joined by highways to Old Faithful, Lake Area, and South Entrance. This portion of **Yellowstone Lake** is called **West Thumb.**

You can marvel at all the thermal features at West Thumb by following the signs along the constructed walks. Chemically, the **Thumb Paint Pots** are similiar to the Fountain Paint Pots at the Lower Geyser Basin. Some consider the colors more vivid. The colors change and the intensity is greater some months than others.

Some of the thermal activity is actually in the lake. **Lakeshore Geyser,** when its crater is not submerged by water, may erupt to heights of 60 feet for several minutes at intervals of 25 to 35 minutes.

Fishing Cone is a hot spring whose geyserite mound and crater are surrounded by lake water. **Abyss Pool,** its deep crater filled with hot, clear water, reflects a remarkable blue color. Abyss Pool vies for popularity with any of the other beautiful pools in the Park. There are numerous distinctly-different hot springs and steam vents of many sizes in the West Thumb area.

Isa Lake, Continental Divide

Geyser Basin, West Thumb

Yellowstone Lake,
West Thumb ▶

Yellowstone Lake ▼

The Lewis River

SOUTH ENTRANCE TO WEST THUMB

Let's assume you are approaching the Park from the south, a 22-mile trip from the South Entrance to West Thumb. You'll leave the startling, towering, majestic peaks of the Grand Tetons as the Rockefeller Memorial Parkway approaches the **South Entrance.** The South Entrance Road begins by the Snake River, at this point only a gently flowing mountain stream with sandy banks. (Farther south in Idaho, it becomes the raging torrent which carved out the fantastic Hell's Canyon and earned it the name, "River of No Return.")

About 1½ miles from the Park entrance, watch for the parking area (easy to miss) where Crawfish Creek forms a spectacular split waterfall—**Moose Falls**—as it tumbles down from the plateau toward the deep canyon of the Lewis River. It's on the east side of the road just north of the bridge over the creek.

The road continues its climb up the edge of **Pitchstone Plateau** to an elevation of 9,000 feet. Pitchstone is a lava ash, a form of rhyolite which was exploded out of the earth during the great volcanic eruptions. The marshy swampland along the adjacent Lewis River is a natural habitat for moose.

After about three miles, the road skirts the very edge of **Lewis River Canyon** where you can peer down for 600 feet between sinister black lava walls. The 37-foot plunge of **Lewis Falls** is next—to the west as the road crosses the Lewis River bridge. There's a parking area next to the bridge where you can get a good view (and take another picture).

A little farther on, the highway follows right along **Lewis Lake** for about 2½ miles, a picture-book lake and a favorite spot for campers and picnickers. (There's a campground at the south end of the lake.) Lewis Lake and Lewis River were named after Captain Lewis of the Lewis and Clark Expedition.

In about six more miles, you'll reach **Grant Village** and the turn-off road to the east. Facilities include Hamilton General Store, Photo Shop, campgrounds , lodging, gift shop, restaurant, marina steak house, boat ramp, ranger station, amphitheater, camper's service building, service station, and post office. The exhibits in the Grant Village Visitor Center give you an excellent introduction to the major features of Yellowstone with emphasis on the wilderness aspects. A slide program is presented each half hour in the auditorium where you may listen to an informative and dramatic reading about our Yellowstone heritage.

Grant Village is but a 2-mile drive to **West Thumb** where you are again back on the Grand Loop. West Thumb got its unusual name because early explorers thought that Yellowstone Lake resembled a hand and this bay looked to them like its thumb.

WEST THUMB TO LAKE JUNCTION

From West Thumb Junction, the Grand Loop Road follows **Yellowstone Lake's** shoreline and abruptly enters a dense spruce and fir forest for about a half-mile. The road following the shoreline affords the opportunity to more fully comprehend the size and beauty of the lake. Yellowstone Lake is the largest lake in North America at this high an elevation, 7,733 feet. It is 20 miles long and 14 miles across from West Thumb to the opposite shore. It covers 139 square miles and has a shoreline of 110 miles. It has an average

Bridge Bay Marina, Yellowstone Lake

Yellowstone Lake from the Grand Loop Road

Fishing Bridge

depth of 139 feet, although it goes as deep as 390 feet. In the lake are **Dot Island, Frank Island, Stevenson Island, Molly Island** (in the southeast arm), and **Peale Island** (in the south arm).

About 19 miles from West Thumb, a road branches to the west and takes you to a natural bridge of stone, 40-feet high with a 30-foot span. This turn-off is only a few yards before you come to the entrance to Bridge Bay Marina. **Bridge Bay Marina,** to the left of the highway, has a small Hamilton Store, boat facilities (rowboats, outboards, inboards, and cabin cruisers), also tour boats, boat ramp, campground and amphitheater.

Lake, as the area is simply called, is a short distance beyond Bridge Bay and has facilities which include a Hamilton General Store, Lake Hospital, hotel, lodge, cottages, post office, service station, and ranger station.

Lake Junction is a three-way junction. The Grand Loop Roads to Canyon Junction and West Thumb are joined by the East Entrance Road.

Fishing Bridge is located near the outlet of Yellowstone Lake. The facilities in this area include a Hamilton General Store and service station, trailer village, self-service laundry, public showers, auto towing and repairs, museum, and ranger station. Because the area is a prime spawning ground, fishing is no longer permitted from Fishing Bridge. The **Fishing Bridge** Museum features exhibits on the wildlife and geology of the Yellowstone Lake area.

During the summer months, it is not unusual to see visitors lined up elbow-to-elbow watching the native Cutthroat Trout beneath the bridge. These trout are so named because of the bright orange or red stripes that slash across their throats. California Gulls are constantly present. Below the bridge a short distance, it is frequently possible to see white pelicans with very long flattened bills. They nest on Molly Island in Yellowstone Lake where they rear their naked young.

EAST ENTRANCE TO LAKE JUNCTION

Many of the eastern and midwestern visitors to Yellowstone come by way of Cody, Wyoming, some 52 miles from the East Entrance. Cody is an enterprising mountain town founded by Col. William F. Cody, better known as Buffalo Bill. Its art center would be a credit to any metropolitan city. The Whitney Gallery, for example, has a splendid collection of western painters and sculptors, including the works of C. M. Russell and Frederick Remington.

Part of the drive from Cody passes through the lush Shoshone National Forest. Other highlights of the trip include Buffalo Bill Dam (328 feet high), and eroded rock pinnacles of fantastic forms such as Chimney Rock, Holy City, and the Palisades.

The **East Entrance Road** inside of the Park offers more beautiful alpine-type scenery than any other road in the Park. You enter at 6,951 feet and climb steadily for seven miles to an exhilarating 8,541 feet and **Sylvan Pass.** The drive is through lodgepole pine forests along Middle Creek until you reach tiny **Eleanor Lake** and, then Sylvan Lake, both at 8,000 feet. Picturesque **Sylvan Lake,** with its winding, wooded shores is worthy of a few minutes' admiration.

Wild hollyhock bushes (Globemallow) with their large clustered pink blossoms decorate your drive. Thimbleberry bushes represent the rose family here with tall plants bearing white flowers that later become berries.

Beyond Sylvan Lake, the road winds down the west sides of the Absaroka Mountains. ("Absaroka" is the Indian name for the Crow Nation, which is curious since these mountains were never Crow territory.) Although the Absaroka Mountains are formed of lava ash, they are not true volcanoes, but the remains of an ancient volcanic plateau carved away by millions of years of erosion.

About 16 miles from the East Gate, take the one-mile side road north to **Lake Butte Overlook**. The overlook is 600 feet above Yellowstone Lake and you'll be rewarded with a breathtaking view of the Lake and the wilderness beyond. On a clear day, you can see—not "forever," but almost—to the snowcapped Teton peaks, some 60 miles to the southwest.

Back on the East Entrance Road, you'll continue along the lake shore and pass near **Steamboat Springs,** with its steam vents and hot springs. (Yellowstone's amazing thermal features are always with you, no matter how varied the terrain.)

Keep a sharp bird's-eye on the sky over the lake for the osprey. These "fish hawks" hover in air currents almost motionlessly as they peer below into the water for fish. Suddenly, one will crash into the water feet first, and then swiftly fly away to his nest, an unhappy fat fish held securely in his talons.

The road next skirts the edge of little **Mary's Bay** and then cuts across an area with swamp ground on both sides. Watch for seagulls, pelicans, ducks, and perhaps a trumpeter swan in the marsh and, ahead, in the waters of **Pelican Creek.**

Just this side of Pelican Creek, the road angles north. You may see a cow moose and her calf. Or, a stately bull may raise his antlered head to show off the curious "bell" which hangs from his throat. This bell is a growth of hide and hair unique to these massive animals.

Beyond the creek, you're back to the Fishing Bridge area again, ready to rejoin the Grand Loop just across the Yellowstone River which drains from Yellowstone Lake.

Yellowstone Lake

Grizzly Bears

Black Bear in Tree ►

Black Bear —
Brown Color Phase ▼

Hamilton's Lake Store

LAKE JUNCTION TO CANYON JUNCTION

From Lake Junction to **Canyon Junction** and **Canyon Village,** the Grand Loop Road follows the Yellowstone River for about 16 miles. Three miles from Lake Junction across the Yellowstone River, you'll see a maze of dead and downed timber. Lodgepole pine trees are shallow-rooted and, consequently, are easily leveled by the wind. When one in an area is uprooted, more usually follow.

Farther on, a short side road leads to a parking area for **Mud Volcano** and other thermal features. This is the moodiest and most evil-looking of all the Park's thermal wonders. The odor of hydrogen sulphide ("rotten eggs") gas pervades the area. The whole region is exciting and awesome with gutteral mud volcanoes, steaming vents, and sizzling, hissing pools. These curious thermal features are produced by the usual factors of surface water which absorbs the heat from the volcanic gases rising from the fiery molten magma below.

The trail to **Black Dragon's Caldron** and back is less than a mile. Black Dragon's Caldron broke out in 1948 with seething masses of pitch black mud in which huge bubbles burst with such unusual force that they flung the sticky rubbery mud into nearby trees. Since that time, the Caldron has shifted some 200 feet from its first area of activity.

Sour Lake is a pool containing acid water which was formed by rising hydrogen sulphide gas which reacted with oxygen in the air to form an acid.

The standing dead trees were killed by the acid water.

The **Mud Volcano,** constantly churning, leaches materials from the lava rock to produce the mud and the gray colors.

The surging, churning, pulsating action at **Dragon's Mouth,** like a fiery dragon's tongue, is generated by explosive bursts of steam which sends the water against the roof of the cavern and out into a run-off channel.

Across the road from the parking area, look carefully and you'll see many small geysers in the Yellowstone River forcing small spurts of hot water above the level of the river.

Sulphur Caldron was aptly named for the free sulphur in its yellow water. **Sizzling Basin** is fascinating because of the hot gases that bubble up through the water. **Grizzly Fumarole** is "hibernating," but could become an active geyser again.

Broad **Hayden Valley,** with the Yellowstone River placidly flowing through it, comes in view as the trip to Canyon Junction continues. This beautiful valley with its rolling hills, large open sagebrush meadows, ponds and marshlands, is a natural wildlife sanctuary. Coyotes range throughout the Valley searching for rodents and other small animals. It is not unusual, especially in the early and late season, to see bison grazing here where food and water are available. Were it not for the great wilderness areas such as Yellowstone where these huge mammals were—and still are—protected, it is doubtful that they could have survived. Incidentally, the calm-looking bison has a very uncertain disposition and should never be approached.

Grizzly bears enjoy the wide open reaches of Hayden Valley, too. They are larger than black bears and have a distinctive hump on their shoulders. Their face is dished in. The grizzly may be black or brown, but there is often a grayish tinge to its fur. Grizzlies use their long claws to dig up rodents and to tear logs apart looking for ants and other insects. They also eat fish, berries, and mammals. If you are fortunate enough to see one, "bear" in mind that their behavior is unpredictable, to say the least. All bears are dangerous, so do not trust any bears, even the cuddly little ones. Mamma is near!

There is a great variety of bird life along the river, its tributaries, and the many small ponds and marshes. The duck varieties are much in evidence. The mallard with its green head frequents the ponds and feeds in the shallow water with its tail up and head down. Barrow's Goldeneye can be spotted in the ponds and shallows of the river. Mergansers are adept at diving and prefer the river water where they obtain their main diet, fish. White Pelicans are easily identified by their long flat yellow bills and their imposing size. Hawks, especially Swainson's Hawk and the Red-tailed Hawk, soar over the meadows. They are predators, and feed on rodents and insects which they can spot very easily with their keen vision. Watch them soar and suddenly dive in pursuit of their prey.

Bison Cow and Calf

◀ *Lower Falls of the Yellowstone*

Upper Falls and Chittenden Bridge

Mt. Washburn, which is reached by the highest road in the Park.

You might be fortunate to observe the Great Blue Heron along the river banks or marshes where they slowly wade and carefully stalk fish, toads, and insects. They usually build their nests in a rookery or colony with other Herons at the tops of tall dead trees in marshy areas such as this. They fly with the neck folded and head drawn into the shoulders. Occasionally, you can also see the Bald Eagle, national bird of the United States.

At **Trout Creek,** observe the peculiar double loop (*monad*) formed by the meandering stream. The imposing mountain ahead and to the right is **Mt. Washburn.** The building on its summit is a fire lookout. (The other two primary fire lookouts are on Mt. Holmes and Mt. Sheridan.)

Below Alum Creek, the Yellowstone River Valley narrows and the river, squeezed tighter, picks up power and speed as if to ready itself for its Herculean task of carving a grand canyon.

To your right is the **Chittenden Bridge** over which a highway leads to **Artist Point** on the south rim of the Grand Canyon of the Yellowstone River. About a mile and a half away, park and follow the foot-trail sign which leads you to a splendid view of the **Upper Falls.** The river, so peaceful and placid flowing through Hayden Valley, suddenly surges over the rock barrier, breaks free with a green crest, and plunges recklessly 109 feet to the river below.

A short walk leads to **Uncle Tom's Trail,** named for Tom Richardson who in 1890 built the first trail into the canyon. The trip down the trail with its steps and resting platforms is an unbelievable, unforgettable experience. (It'll take your breath away, in more ways than one!) The thundering plunge of the **Lower Falls** drops 308 feet and sends a foamy, misty spray against the green moss walls of the canyon. From the canyon in late morning and early afternoon, the sun reflects a colorful rainbow in the spray. If the wind currents are right, the spray mist may reach you at the bottom of the trail.

Before ascending the few steps to view the canyon at **Artist Point,** read the material in the exhibit to better understand the formation of the canyon. The view of the Lower Falls and Canyon from Artist Point is a favorite of Yellowstone visitors. The canyon walls are predominantly yellow, but blue, red, orange, and brown are also present. The colors are due to altered rhyolite rock and the oxides of its minerals, especially iron. The colors are everchanging, and the sunshine after rains intensifies them to even more spectacular hues and contrasts.

If you'll look carefully upstream on the left canyon wall only a few yards above the river, you may see a geyser in eruption, or steam issuing from its opening. It erupts at an angle toward the river. There is evidence that at one time, before the mighty Yellowstone River carved out the canyon, this was a thermal area with hot springs and geysers.

It was the yellow coloring that gave the area the name Yellowstone. *"The Story of Man in Yellowstone"* by Merril D. Beal reveals the following in part:

The Minnetaree Indian name for the river was Mitsia-dazi, which means Rock Yellow River. The French equivalent, Roche Jaune, was also in common use among the Indians and trappers, although when or by whom the name was given is unknown. American trappers called the river "Yallerstone."

A foot trail to **Point Sublime** rewards the hiker with another spectacular view of the canyon and the river far below.

Page 54: Lower Falls of the Yellowstone River ►
Page 55: Grand Canyon and Lower Falls from Artist Point ►

Return to the Grand Loop Road by the same highway and cross the Chittenden Bridge. Turn right on the Grand Loop and continue to Canyon Junction and Canyon Village where the following facilities are available: Hamilton General Store, Hamilton Photo Shop, service station, visitor center, ranger station, post office, restaurant, cafeteria, cabins, public campground (only for hard-sided vehicles), self-service laundry, and amphitheater.

It is suggested that you stop at the visitor center for orientation. Observe the exhibits and diagrams which explain the origin of Yellowstone's Grand Canyon and display some of the plants and animals that live along its rim. Ask one of the ranger naturalists at the information desk about the schedule of naturalist activities. They can also explain how to get to Inspiration Point, Glacial Boulder, Grand View, Lookout Point, and Red Rock.

The views are fascinating and spectacular from any of the observation points on either the north or south rim. Yet each is different. To take the **North Rim Drive,** continue up the Grand Loop to Canyon Village and turn east at the intersection. The road passes between the campground and the visitor center. In about a mile, it divides. To the left is a two-way road that dead-ends at Inspiration Point. To the right is the one-way North Rim Drive.

Inspiration Point emphasizes the magnitude of the canyon which is 24 miles long and from 800 to 1200 feet deep, and has two waterfalls that total a 417-foot drop.

At **Lookout Point** and **Red Rock Point,** the views of the Canyon and the Lower Falls to some visitors surpass the view from Artist Point. Each view is breathtaking.

From several viewpoints along the north rim drive, you can see ospreys' nests perched upon inaccessible rock pinnacles. Ospreys mate for life and return to the same nest year after year. The nest of sticks looks like a brush-pile. Ospreys are often mistaken for eagles.

Violet-green swallows are common in Yellowstone's Grand Canyon. They are graceful fliers, which helps since they feed almost entirely on flying insects. You can watch them best from Lookout Point as they dart to and from their nests or crannies located on the canyon walls.

CANYON JUNCTION TO NORRIS JUNCTION

Canyon Junction on the Grand Loop Road leads to **Norris Junction** (12 miles) and to **Tower Junction** (19 miles).

The first few miles toward Norris Junction pass through a lodgepole pine forest. Since the forest is very dense, the trees must grow rapidly to reach sunlight. The slower-growing trees are suppressed and, since they cannot obtain sunlight, they die. The lower limbs of the growing trees are pruned by Nature, since they cannot obtain enough light. The density results in tall,

Lodgepole Pine Forest

straight trees. The Indians used the tall, slender poles in the construction of lodges and tepee conical tents—hence the name lodgepole.

The lodgepole pine trees have naturally reseeded road banks where recent road construction has occurred. The winged seeds from the cones of nearby trees germinate and grow into young trees in a few years.

About three miles from Norris Junction, a short one-way scenic loop (toward Canyon Junction) leads to **Virginia Cascades.** In this narrow rocky canyon, the Gibbon River glides into the canyon opening and slips like a lacy veil over smooth rocks 60 feet below. The picturesque setting affords an ideal environment for thrush-type water birds called ouzels.

Above and below the canyon, the large meadows are inhabited by elk (Wapiti), most often seen during early morning and early evening hours.

Yellow Monkeyflower
◄ *Autumn Aspen Trees*

Indian Paintbrush, Wyoming State Flower

Moose and Calf

CANYON JUNCTION TO TOWER JUNCTION

At Canyon Junction, the Grand Loop Road begins its climb up at Washburn Range and over Dunraven Pass (8,859 feet) to Tower Junction.

The trip from Canyon Junction on the flank of Mt. Washburn to Tower Junction is one of delightful, unending variety. Throughout your trip around the Park, you have observed such plant communities as sagebrush grasslands, grassy meadows, lodgepole pine forests, spruce and fir forests. You noted that each community supported different forms of animal life. This segment is one where plant and animal zones come into even sharper focus. If you walk to the summit of Mt. Washburn, you will find the white-bark pine at timberline, gnarled, twisted, and wind-whipped. Below timberline, the spruce and fir are dwarfed and look like shrubs. The animal species at or near timberline are few, but include Bighorn Sheep, marmots, and pika.

Lodgepole pine is the dominant species for the first few miles, but with an increase in elevation, spruce and fir find moisture from melting snow conducive to growth. Huge fir snow mats and flowers in brilliant colors cover mountainsides. The balsamroot with yellow flowers and large basal leaves are conspicuous. Along the roads where water seepage is provided, brilliant red monkeyflowers flourish. Alpine forget-me-nots with their densely-clustered blue flowers blanket the mountains.

You can sometimes see black bears along the road. Various color phases may occur—black, brown, and cinnamon. They are smaller than grizzly bears and do not have the hump over the shoulders. They are omnivorous and, in their natural habitat, eat grass, berries, fruits, insects, fish, and carrion.

At **Dunraven Pass** at an elevation of 8,859 feet (the highest elevation on the entire Grand Loop Road), a foot trail about 3.6 miles long leads to the summit of **Mt. Washburn.** A foot trail climbing Mt. Washburn also leaves from the Chrittenden parking area, located on the north side of Mt. Washburn. The rewards are many for the hiker. The rocky crags constitute the summer range for the Bighorn Sheep. At the summit on a clear day, much of Yellowstone National Park is spread out before you in all its glory. A hundred miles away, the Teton Mountains are clearly visible, and the mountain ranges within the Park are easily identified. Yellowstone Lake, the Yellowstone River, and parts of the Grand Canyon are a part of the panorama. Steam puffs here and there indicate areas of thermal activity. The immensity of forest coverage and its great watershed become more meaningful when viewed from this vantage point. At the summit, the elevation is 10,243 feet. You can't help but admire the tenacity with which plants and animals at this elevation struggle to exist in spite of great odds.

Leaving Dunraven Pass, the highway continues to the northern base of Mt. Washburn. No private cars are permitted to travel to the summit. The sweeping view from the summit is well worth the hike. Take a warm jacket, rain gear and drinking water. Postpone your trip if a storm is threatening.

The highway continues to the **Tower Fall** area where there is a large parking area and restrooms. Hamilton's General Store provides groceries, food service, books, gifts, souvenirs, postcards, and photo supplies. Tower Fall campground, a half-mile away, has campsites with running water, tables, restrooms, and amphitheater.

Beyond the guard rail at the parking area, the children will enjoy watching the little ground squirrels, also called "picket-pins" or Uinta Ground Squirrels (*Kennicott spermophile*).

A short distance from the parking area, a trail leads to a platform overlooking **Tower Fall** on Tower Creek with cascades 132 feet to the rocks below. Foot trails extend to the foot of the fall and **Undercliff Springs.**

Pronghorn

◄ *Tower Fall*

Petrified Tree, Near Tower Junction

Along the road to Tower Junction are turnouts to permit leisurely views of natural features. The canyon is 500 feet deep in some places.

Across the gorge on the canyon wall, you'll see what appears to be palisades or stockades. The geologic past of the area is presented on the wall in seven layers once built up under an inland sea:

1. Breccia (fragmental rocks consisting of larger particles than ash or tuff formed by volcanic debris with angular fragments cemented together.)
2. Steam gravels
3. Basalt lava cooled in pentagonal forms
4. Stream gravels and sediments
5. Lava flow of five-sided basalt forms
6. Lake deposits
7. Glacial drifts

Overhanging Cliff rests on gravel and fine stream deposits with columnar basalt exposed above which is rhyolite. Overhanging Cliff actually does hang over the road.

The **Needle** is a spire of volcanic breccia 260 feet high and was caused by erosion.

The mysterious-looking **Narrows** is the narrowest part of the entire Yellowstone Canyon, but is 500 feet deep.

Thermal activity in the Grand Canyon area is revealed by steam issuing from fumaroles, steam vents, and hot springs. Among these are **Calcite Springs** where calcite, gypsum, and sulphur are deposited by the hot waters.

A ranger station, service station, and Roosevelt Lodge are part of the Tower Junction area. A Hamilton Photo Shop is located next to **Roosevelt Lodge.** The Lodge is located on a short loop road from Tower Junction and was named for President Theodore Roosevelt who camped nearby around the turn of the century.

Naturalist activities include an evening campfire talk. If you are interested in an all-day hike, the fossil forest hike to the **Petrified Forests** on Specimen Ridge is recommended. (Check at any visitor center as to when the next conducted walk is scheduled.)

NORTHEAST ENTRANCE TO TOWER JUNCTION

If you're approaching Yellowstone from the northeastern corner, you'll drive through the old mining towns of Cooke City and Silver Gate. They are tucked protectively at the base of spectacular **Beartooth Range** and the highway enters the Park right on the state line between Montana and Wyoming.

Cooke City was a gold and silver mining town which began in 1873, a year after Yellowstone became a National Park. The **Republic Mountain** (10,170 feet) enhances the natural setting of the town. From Cooke City, hike up to the unusual Grasshopper Glacier on Iceberg Peak where millions of grasshoppers were caught and quick-frozen in the ice.

This is all "Big Sky Country," with panoramic views, mighty mountains and valley lakes, a timberline vegetation that's stunted and gnarled but cheerful with the bright colors of wildflowers.

Inside the Northeast Entrance Gate, the highway takes you along **Soda Butte Creek** with the **Absaroka Mountains** towering above you. You'll pass between two of the Park's highest peaks, **Abiathar Peak** (10,928) to the east and **Barronette Peak** (10,404) to the west.

An interesting stop, eleven miles into the Park, will be **Soda Butte** on your left-hand side. This fascinating terrace of calcium carbonate was formed by the hot waters of its spring which dissolved the limestone and brought it out of the earth. The dead terrace has no color of its own, but the algae living in the warm water turn it into a rainbow of hues and shadings.

The road then leaves the narrower valley and enters the **Lamar River Valley** whose broad open meadows were created by a great glacier 10,000 or more years ago during the last Ice Age. Granite glacial boulders are scattered over the terrain. Notice that near almost all of the boulders just one tree is growing. A seed found a desirable place to germinate and, once its seedling started to grow, it was protected—particularly from the wind—by the boulder. Moisture held under the boulder, and shade from it, helped the seedling survive and flourish.

Bison, elk, and Pronghorn graze in the expansive meadows. The Pronghorn Antelope are easily identified by their tawny color, large white rump patch, white bands on their throat, and white underparts. The Lamar Valley is also a good area to watch for Canada geese, ducks, and the other members of Yellowstone's water fowl family.

Toward the end of your 29 miles from the Northeast Gate to the Grand Loop, you'll pass through the narrower Lamar Canyon. The huge granite boulders in the Canyon were carried here by glaciers.

To the south is Specimen Ridge which you'll also encounter on the trip from Canyon Junction to Tower Junction. The north slopes of **Specimen Ridge** reveal numerous petrified trees exposed in the upright position exactly where they grew millions of years ago. Geologists have identified 9 to 12 separate petrified forests on the cliffside, one on top of the other.

The road joins the Grand Loop across from the entrance roadway to the Roosevelt Lodge.

Bison Herd

Bison Bull

Moose Bull Feeding

Elk in Summer

TOWER JUNCTION TO MAMMOTH HOT SPRINGS

Tower Junction to **Mammoth Hot Springs** is a pleasant 18-mile trip down another beautiful valley.

Douglas Fir Trees are common in the Tower Fall area where the 6,270-foot elevation is favorable for their growth. The cones are characterized by the three-pronged bracts which protrude between the scales and give a fringed appearance. Aspen trees grow in groves around ponds and on hillsides where they can take advantage of the water seepage.

A spur road, about a mile from Roosevelt Lodge, leads a mile and a half to the **Petrified Tree.** (Because of its limited parking area, no trailers are permitted on the spur.) The Petrified Tree—a stump really—is enclosed by a tall iron fence, and stands in the same spot where it grew in a redwood forest millions of years ago. At one time, several tree stumps were in the same vicinity, and all but this one were carried away by "human erosion." Visitors collected specimens until only this one remained. There is no doubt that it would have met the same fate had it not been fenced in. It is now possible for visitors of today, and those of future generations, to observe and wonder at this geological rarity. It is contrary to regulations to take any rock specimen out of the Park. Remember the slogan: "Take only pictures—leave only footprints."

Another spur loop road, known as the **Blacktail Plateau Drive,** leaves the Grand Loop Road about nine miles from **Tower Junction.** If you're one of those who enjoys a wayside road to observe wildflowers and other natural delights away from traffic, this is a delightful trip. Make certain as to the direction of travel since this is a one-way road.

North from Elk Creek on the Grand Loop Road between Tower Junction and Mammoth Hot Springs, the grooved and wrinkled **Garnet Hill** looms into view. It is of special interest to amateur geologists since its rocks are among the oldest on earth. They are Precambrian granite gneiss which contain imperfect garnets. This Archean Precambrian granite is said to be **2.7 billion** years old.

Small lakes and ponds are numerous out in the open areas. While beavers are rare in Yellowstone, evidence of former beaver activity is indicated by beaver dams and the cut aspen stumps surrounding the ponds.

Past Blacktail Pond on the north and near Lava Creek is a parking area. Stop there and take the short walk to **Wraith Falls.** Follow the road that crosses the creek and admire **Undine Falls** which drops 60 feet between perpendicular canyon walls.

Bunsen Peak, Mt. Everts, and **Terrace Mountain** silhouette the skyline. Bunsen Peak was named after the first scientist who theorized the action of geysers (the inventor of the famous Bunsen burner). The **Mammoth Hot Springs,** with a background of white, affords an overall view quite different from the usual close-up survey. The road continues over the Sheepeater Canyon Bridge to Mammoth Hot Springs.

NORTH ENTRANCE TO MAMMOTH HOT SPRINGS

The North Entrance Road comes into the Park through the impressive **Roosevelt Arch** (dedicated by President Theodore Roosevelt in 1903). The Arch is inscribed "For the Benefit and Enjoyment of the People."

Just before you reach the checking station and the Arch, you might want to "visit for a spell" in adjoining Gardiner, Montana, an interesting western town well supplied with motels, restaurants, and other traveler comforts. Gardiner is located on Highway 89 which joins Interstate 90 at Livingston, Montana, 56 miles to the north.

Through the Arch and into the Park, the road immediately enters the **Gardner Canyon,** carved to a depth of 600 feet in some parts by the Gardner River. (The spelling is different from the town of Gardiner and, just to make it more confusing, the Gardner River joins the Yellowstone River near Gardiner, Montana.)

The Canyon runs between **Mount Everts** on the east and **Sepulchre Mountain,** so named because of an unusual rock formation resembling a funeral bier. The **Gallatin Mountains** to the west were carved and recarved by glacial action during the last Ice Age. Eagle Nest Rock in the Gardner Canyon was named for the nest of an osprey family (not that of an eagle, despite its name), but the nest fell as a result of an earth tremor several years ago and is no longer there.

Steam rises from **Boiling River** on the bank of the Gardner at the foot of Mount Everts. The hot water from Boiling River flows from beneath a rock ledge and some experts believe that this is an outlet from the Mammoth Hot Springs.

The highway winds back and forth across the river, passes the state line between Montana and Wyoming about three miles into the Park, and soon drops you in the middle of the grey stone buildings of **Mammoth Hot Springs.**

The total trip from the Arch to the Junction: a very interesting five miles.

MAMMOTH HOT SPRINGS TO NORRIS JUNCTION

Mammoth was the first settlement in Yellowstone Park. The Horace M. Albright Visitor Center, open all year, houses exhibits on the history of Yellowstone, its animals and birds, and includes an interesting slide program on the Park's ecology, philosophy and history. Information, books,

Theodore Roosevelt Arch, North Entrance

Gardner River

Albright Visitor Center at Mammoth Village

Elk Feeding

and permits may be obtained from Park personnel. From the front porch of the visitor center, the Mammoth Hot Springs are spread before you, a wonderland of white and brightly-colored terraces on the flanks of Terrace Mountain. Most of the buildings are part of historic Fort Yellowstone, built by the U.S. Army during its 30-year administration of the Park.

Other facilities include the Hamilton General Store and Photo Shop, Christmas Shop, service station, hotel, cabins, fast food restaurant, campground, auto towing and repair, saddle horses, superintendent's office, medical clinic, post office, and amphitheater.

The Grand Loop Road between Mammoth and Norris passes the base of the lower group of springs. A self-guiding nature trail explains the hydrothermal activities to be seen from the boardwalks.

During the summer season, Park Service Naturalists guide walks among the terraces and to other interesting areas here and throughout the Park. Look for a list of Ranger led activities at all visitor centers.

The first attraction, driving toward the hot springs, is the **Liberty Cap,** an ancient natural statue 37 feet high and 20 feet in diameter at the base. It is a cone composed of calcium carbonate, deposited at a time when hot water flowed from the opening at its top.

The **Upper Terraces** of the world-famous Mammoth Hot Springs may be reached by car on a one-way road off the Grand Loop Road which circles the terraces and hot springs for a mile and a half and then rejoins the Grand Loop. This road is too narrow and winding for trailers and buses.

The terraces and hot springs are an excellent example of the "living geology" seen throughout the Park. Nature carries on a great mining project in which hot water transports a form of limestone to the surface where it is deposited like so much sugar frosting to build and decorate the terraces. The hot springs and their terraces are constantly changing. Springs which were active last year may be inactive or dormant this year. A new spring may break out at any time. For example, people who visited the area before the early 1930's frequently referred to the dazzling white color of Angel Terrace as hot water flowed over its surface. Angel Terrace is now active again.

It has been estimated that two tons of dissolved limestone are brought to the surface of the terraces each day. Roughly 500 gallons of water per minute flow from the springs. This flow has been approximately the same since the springs have been studied.

Water collects on a series of steps, enhancing the beautiful **Upper Terrace** and its series of basin-like pools. When the top basin is filled, the water flows over the lip and drips down to successive basins below. The hot water is literally turning the mountain inside out. Algae grows in the hot water, creating delicate pastel shades. (The temperature of the water that algae is growing in determines its color.)

In recent years, the most active hot springs have been **Opal, Orange Spring Mound, Minerva,** and **Jupiter.** However, you could return year after year and be aware—and amazed—at the changes. No one can predict which area on the terraces will be active next year. It's obvious that Nature is dynamic—not static!

On the Upper Terraces, you'll see gnarled and twisted trees with scale-like leaves called Rocky Mountain Juniper. Though small, these Junipers are considered by many experts to be the oldest living forms of life in the Park. You instinctively have to admire their tenacity in the struggle to survive.

When you leave the Terraces to join the Grand Loop Road, notice the beautiful grove of aspen trees along the highway. The aspen, which turn beautiful colors in the fall, are the most common of the relatively few broad-leafed trees in the Park.

Proceeding southward toward Norris Junction along the winding road, you'll approach **Silver Gate** and the **Hoodoos.** In pre-glacial time, hot springs on Terrace Mountain deposited a thick layer of travertine. A great landslide, long before the Park was established, brought down huge boulders from the travertine layer which came to rest in the jumble to be seen today.

The **Golden Gate** and the canyon walls on both sides of **Golden Gate Canyon** owe their color to yellow lichens which thrive on the bare, exposed rocks. Golden Gate Canyon and the surrounding area were considerably damaged as a result of successive tremors from the Madison Canyon earthquake of 1959. The Golden Gate Canyon Road was blocked, as were several other roads in the Park, because of rock debris resulting from massive slides. Many hot springs and geysers were changed; some becoming more active, some less . . . some went dormant. New geysers, hot springs, fumaroles, solfatara, and steam vents were created by deep-seated tremors. Underground, new fissures, tubes, and cracks resulted from the jarring tremors and the superheated waters and steam found new access to the surface.

If you are curious about earthquakes, volcanism, and glaciation, stop at visitor centers and museums at Norris, Canyon, and Fishing Bridge where the Park's geological history is on display. Rangers will answer your questions; and exhibits, slide programs, and specific publications will further your understanding of Yellowstone geology.

In this picturesque setting of Golden Gate, **Rustic Falls** drops its veil of water 47 feet into the canyon. Beyond the fall, **Swan Lake Flat** opens out, silhouetted by the Gallatin Mountains to the west. To the east, an old one way road goes around the base of Bunsen Peak; it begins at the northern end of Swan Lake Flats and travels north-northeast to the old CC camp. It follows the edge of the 800-foot deep **Sheepeater Canyon** of the Gardner River, and affords exciting views of Osprey Falls. A trail leads to the base of the falls and another trail, beginning where the Bunsen Peak road leaves

Main Terrace, Mammoth

Angel Terrace, Mammoth

Rocky Mountain Big Horn Sheep

Minerva Terrace, Mammoth

the Grand Loop, leads to the top of the peak for sweeping views of the surrounding mountains and plateaus.

The Bunsen Peak road rejoins the Grand Loop Road just below the Upper Terrace Loop Drive.

Back at Rustic Falls, the vista opens to reveal **Swan Lake Flat** where several species of sagebrush (Artemisia) dominate the landscape. Leaving Kingman Pass and Rustic Falls, you can't help but be impressed with the view of the dominating peak to the north. The mountain so bold and conspicuous is **Electric Peak** with an elevation of 10,992 feet. Once thought to be the highest mountain in Yellowstone, it was later proved that Eagle Peak (11,360 feet) in the southeast corner of the Park is, indeed, the highest.

Westward, the rugged Gallatin Mountain Range includes **Mt. Holmes** (10,300 feet), **Quadrant Mountain, Antler Peak, Dome Mountain,** and **White Peaks.**

Swan Lake, near the road, occasionally rewards the Park visitor with a view of its priceless inhabitants, the majestic trumpeter swans. These birds find a haven in the Yellowstone sanctuary almost as if they knew they were protected by law.

Before crossing the **Gardner River,** a short road leads to **Sheepeater Cliffs** made up of basalt-column piles or posts. The molten volcanic rock cooled to form these pentagonal and hexagonal columns. The Sheepeater Indians lived in this area.

The environment favored by moose is along lakes, ponds, swampland, and river bottoms where various shrubs grow. They are especially fond of willow shrubs and the various underwater plants. The moose found in Yellowstone is the impressive Shiras which has palmate antlers. (Palmate means "resembling a hand with the fingers spread.") The bulls may weight up to 1,000 pounds, which is exactly half a ton.

Obsidian Cliff, Jim Bridger's famous "Mountain of Glass," is certainly worthy of inspection. Chemically, this rock formation is the same as rhyolite, but—in this case—the rhyolite cooled so quickly that it did not crystalize. Instead, "black glass" was formed. The cliff is approximately 200 feet high. Indians made utensils which, with age and rediscovery, are considered artifacts. No specimens may be collected.

Note the beaver dams at **Beaver Lake.**

Roaring Mountain (8,000 feet) is interesting to see because of its steaming and hissing vents. This area was once probably a major scene of hot spring activity. The mountain is named for a single vent that roared for months in 1902 during the outburst of intense activity.

Lemonade Lake, so named for its lemon-lime color, is also interesting if only for the naked dead trees standing erect in the water.

Drive slowly to observe the lakes, hot springs, forests, and flowers on both sides of the road. Note **Frying Pan Spring** with is numerous vents which open into shallow water to release its various hot gases.

Dark Cavern Geyser, Norris Geyser Basin

NORRIS JUNCTION TO MADISON JUNCTION

From Norris Junction, the highway to the east leads to **Canyon Junction** and the highway southwest, to Madison Junction. At Norris Junction, there is a museum, and campground, but no stores or lodging. Look for the road which leaves the Grand Loop Road for Norris Geyser Basin parking area to the west.

The **Geyser Basins** announce themselves almost at once by the rising steam and familiar pungent odor of hydrogen sulphide. Discover the highlights of the area by picking up a self-guiding brochure at the Norris Museum. Schedules for guided walks and some geyser eruptions are posted on bulletin boards. Geyser activity is far from predictable, and the following information is subject to change almost as you watch.

As has been mentioned, when you're looking over a geyser basin, you'll notice a characteristic light gray mineral material. Unlike the travertine at Mammoth, the material here is silicon dioxide, a hydrous form of quartz called geyserite, or siliceous sinter. The siliceous sinter is held in solution in the geyser and hot spring water, and deposited at a much slower rate than travertine. Geyser cones are made of this material.

Of the more than 10,000 thermal features in the Park, many varieties are located in the Norris Geyser Basin. **Steamboat Geyser** was once the most powerful geyser in Yellowstone. When it erupted in its major phase, the water reached heights of 400 feet! Unfortunately for today's camera-buffs, its last major eruption was on October 4, 1991.

Liberty Cap at Mammoth Hot Springs

Golden Gate Bridge Near Mammoth

Gibbon Falls

Grizzly Bear

Echinus Geyser is a magnificent, spectacular geyser erupting to heights of 75 feet at intervals varying between 50 and 60 minutes with a duration of 5 to 14 minutes. Sulphur and arsenic are deposited here by some of the thermal features. There are roaring and hissing steam vents (fumaroles) and solfatara depositing sulphur around their vents.

Among the more unusual natural features is **Cinder Pool,** on whose surface float tiny little gray-black hollow balls said to be composed of iron pyrite and sulphur. The pulsating hot water on the surface washes the balls into run-off channels.

From the parking area at the Norris Geyser Basin, the road rejoins the Grand Loop road to **Madison Junction** following the Gibbon River. Across the river are the **Chocolate Pots** which are brown in color, caused not by algae, but by iron (ferric oxide), and siliceous sinter in solution in the hot water gurgling out of their openings.

At the **Artist Paint Pot** the parking area is located on the east side of the road at the southern end of Gibbon Meadows. A short trail leads to the colorful **Paint Pots.** Keep a sharp eye out over Elk Park and Gibbon Meadows for grazing elk.

Across the Gibbon River Bridge on the west bank is a one-mile foot trail that leads (up a steep grade) to **Monument Geyser Basin** where many thermos-bottle-shaped geysers perform for visitors.

The highway continues past several interesting hot springs, including **Beryl Spring.**

Gibbon Falls is but one of numerous waterfalls within the Park. Shimmering, veil-like, the water glides over the worn rock except for the far channel where the water spurts turbulently as from a water wheel. The tumbling water drops 84 feet.

As you approach Madison Junction, take time to see **Terrace Spring** with its startlingly beautiful algal colors. Across the road is Purple Mountain whose summit, reached by foot trail, offers a most rewarding view of the surrounding country. From this trail, you can easily and clearly see the confluence of the Gibbon and Firehole Rivers as they join to form the Madison River.

Driving the roads and walking short trails are the best way to start learning about Yellowstone. To learn more about this rare place, it is hoped you can visit often and stay longer.

If you started your journey of the Park at the West entrance—as was the case with this guidebook—you have now completed the 142-mile Grand Loop. The rest of the book contains handy information about the flora, fauna, and some of the necessary man-made rules and regulations.

Reference Materials, Descriptions, Explanations

●

BRIEF HISTORY OF YELLOWSTONE NATIONAL PARK

By Aubrey L. Haines, former Park Historian

In the truest sense, the history of this Park covers only a little more than 150 years, for our written record had its origin in the vague information Indians gave explorers as Lewis and Clark were toiling up the Missouri River on their journey across the continent.

And yet, men had lived on the Yellowstone Plateau for a very long time. A projectile point unearthed a few miles from Park headquarters indicates that, as long as 5,000 years ago, Indians may have hunted where the town of Gardiner, Montana now stands. The ancient campsites and stone articles discovered at many points within the Park, and in the mountains and valleys around it, hint strongly that men have lived here for most of the 8,500 years since the last Ice Age.

At the opening of the historic period, the only Indians making their home in the Park area were the "Sheepeaters" (named for their staple food, not their tribe). They were a mixed group of Shoshone and Bannock Indians who lacked the horses and guns necessary to compete with their neighbors; and thus had retreated into the mountains to live furtive, impoverished lives, even by Indian standards.

John Colter, a fur trapper, appears to have been the first white man to see this land of hot springs and geysers. He probably passed through it during the winter of 1807-08, while searching for Indian customers for a trading post established by Manuel Lisa, lower down on the Yellowstone River. The fur trade flourished briefly in the Rocky Mountains, bringing such men as Jim Bridger, Joe Meek, Daniel Potts, Osborne Russell, and Warren Angus Ferris into the area which is now Yellowstone Park; but a growing scarcity

Pages 82, 83: Old Faithful Geyser ▶

of fine furs, coupled with changes in fashion, brought the fur trade to an end about 1840. The trapper disappeared from the Yellowstone Plateau, and it remained a nearly-forgotten wilderness.

The discovery of gold in neighboring Montana a little more than twenty years later brought exploring parties of miners to the upper Yellowstone country. The time was 1863 and in the years that followed, mining activity established a chain of crude settlements and isolated claims up the Yellowstone and Lamar Rivers to the headwaters of the Clark's Fork River. Some of the knowledge which had been commonplace to John Colter and the fur-trappers was rediscovered and interest in the geyser regions was rekindled.

In 1869, a different type of exploration, based on curiosity rather than profit, began. The first group to come into Yellowstone country for the sole purpose of seeing what it contained was the Folsom-Cook-Peterson party, and the information brought back led to a more thorough exploration by the Washburn-Langford-Doane party in the following year. The writing and lecturing done by members of this second expedition resulted in an official exploration by the United States Geological Survey of the Territories in 1871. From that came a recognition of the Yellowstone "wonders," and, in 1872, the Congress of the United States was perrsuaded to set aside a vast area of 2.4 million acres as *The Yellowstone National Park.*

The new Park was placed in the care of a superintendent. Without funds for its maintenance and without laws for its protection, he could not accomplish what was expected of him. The four superintendents who followed him were likewise incapable of adequately developing and protecting the Park. Thus, the job of managing it for the nation was given, finally, to the United States Army.

From 1886 until 1917, that trust was ably administered. The necessary public works were completed by officers of the Corps of Engineers, while soldiers stationed at key points brought respect for law and order with the assistance of hardy scouts. Thirty-two years of brusque but fair administration corrected the early abuses so that civilian management could be tried again.

A new organization, the National Park Service, was authorized by Congress on August 25, 1916. Under it, the Park was administered by a superintendent, assisted by a corps of rangers who had the powers of civilian policemen. The new form of management has proved satisfactory through the intervening years to the present, allowing Yellowstone National Park to serve the people of this nation as an unrivaled vacationland; a place where they may see some of nature's grandest works, enjoy wholesome, refreshing outdoor activities, and leave with their spirits lifted and their viewpoints broadened. The proof that it has been a worthwhile venture lies in the marvelous growth of the National Park System in this country, and its influence throughout the world.

YELLOWSTONE NATIONAL PARK

THE CONTINENTAL UNITED STATES

LOCATION OF YELLOWSTONE NATIONAL PARK

Yellowstone National Park is located in the Rocky Mountains. Most of it is cached in the northwestern corner of Wyoming. The western boundary reaches into Montana and Idaho, and the northern boundary extends into southern Montana. Yellowstone is surrounded by rugged mountain ranges—Beartooth to the north and the Absaroka to the east. The spectacular Gallatin Mountains border the northwest portion of the Park; and the lofty Teton Range, with its snowcapped peaks, is to the south.

National Forests surround the Park. Gallatin National Forest is along the north and northwest boundaries. Custer National Forest borders Yellowstone on the northeast. The Targhee National Forest borders the west and southwest. Teton National Forest borders the south, and the Shoshone National Forest joins the eastern boundary.

Yellowstone National Park is essentially an elevated plateau hemmed in by lofty snowcapped mountains. The average elevation in the Park is 7,500 feet. Within its boundaries are 3,472 square miles, or almost two-and-one-quarter million acres (2,219,822.70), snaked diagonally by the Continental Divide. It is an area which nature generously lavished with an unbelievable variety of natural phenomena and abundant natural wildlife.

Sunset at Yellowstone River

TRAVEL INFORMATION

There are five main entrances to Yellowstone National Park. Excellent highways lead to each entrance. The chart below indicates when each entrance gate is open and the highways to reach them.

Gate	Access Road	Open
North	via Livingston* and Gardiner, Montana (I.S. 90, U.S. 10 & 89)	All year
West	via West Yellowstone, Montana (U.S. 20 & 191)	May 1 - Oct. 30
South	via Jackson, Wyoming, and Grand Teton National Park* (U.S. 26, 89, 187 & 287)	May 1 - Oct. 30
East	via Cody, Wyoming (U.S. 14, 16 & 20)	May 1 - Oct. 30

The west, south and east gates are opened to snowcoach and snowmobile only from approximately December 15th to March 15th.

| Northeast | via Billings, Red Lodge, and Cooke City,* Montana (I.S. 90, U.S. 10 & 212) | Approx. June 1-Sept. 30 |

*Yellowstone Park Co. buses pick up and discharge passengers at these locations.

Between October 31 and May 1, the Park roads and entrances (except the North Entrance) are closed due to snow. Except for Mammoth, where camping is available all year, most of the Park campgrounds do not open before June.

Commercial Transportation

- Airlines provide year-round service to Idaho Falls, Idaho; Bozeman, Montana; Billings, Montana; and Jackson, Wyoming. In the summer, service is also available to West Yellowstone, Montana, and Cody, Wyoming.
- Major bus lines serve Bozeman, Livingston, West Yellowstone, and Billings, Montana; and Cody and Jackson, Wyoming.
- TW Recreational Services, Inc. provide bus tours of the park's major features and facilities.

Accommodations

Within Yellowstone, there are hotels, lodges, cabins, and the Fishing Bridge Trailer Village. These accommodations are open from mid-June to Labor Day. Limited accommodations are available during the off-season, with winter activities centering around Old Faithful and Mammoth Hot Springs Hotel.

Reservations are advised, especially during July and August. Write to: TW Recreational Services, Inc., Yellowstone National Park, Wyoming 82190. Visitors already in Yellowstone can make advance room reservations anywhere in the Park at any hotel or lodge. You may also make reservations by calling (307) 344-7311.

Adjacent Facilities

There are superb recreational opportunities in the five national forests bordering Yellowstone. Neighboring communities offer complete accommodations and services (many of these are mentioned in the text of the guide book). In addition, many concessioner and Federal facilities are located in the Grand Teton National Park, south of Yellowstone.

HOTELS, INNS, CABINS AND SERVICES

Services and Locations	Suites	Rooms with Bath	Rooms without Bath	Western Cabins	Frontier Cabins	Family Cabins	Budget Cabins	Roughrider Cabins	Rustic Shelters	Dining Room	Cafeteria	Snack Shop/Fast Food	Beverage Lounge	Gift Shop	Beauty Shop
Lake Yellowstone Hotel	•	•	•		•	•				•			•	•	•
Lake Lodge				•	•						•	•	•	•	
Old Faithful Inn	•	•	•							•		•	•	•	•
Old Faithful Snow Lodge (open in winter)			•	•	•					•				•	
Old Faithful Lodge					•			•			•	•		•	
Mammoth Hot Springs Hotel (hotel open in winter)	•	•	•		•		•			•		•	•	•	
Canyon Lodge				•	•					•	•	•	•	•	•
Roosevelt Lodge					•	•		•	•	•					
Grant Village AAA Rated		•								•				•	•

GENERAL STORES, TACKLE SHOPS AND PHOTO SHOPS

Although Yellowstone's primitive beauty and rugged setting surround visitors at every turn, the convenience of a Hamilton Store or Photo Shop is always close at hand. Whether you need film, groceries, fishing tackle or a souvenir of your visit, you'll find all you need and more at a Hamilton Store or Photo Shop. Watch for them as you tour the Park.

	Camping Supplies	Apparel	Sundries	Photo Supplies	Fishing Tackle	Food Service	Gifts and Souvenirs	Groceries	Ice	Indian Handcraft	Liquor & Beverages
Bridge Bay	•	•	•	•	•	•	•	•	•		•
Canyon Village	•	•	•	•	•	•	•	•	•	•	•
Fishing Bridge	•	•	•	•	•	•	•	•	•	•	•
Grant Village	•	•	•	•	•	•	•	•	•	•	•
Lake	•	•	•	•	•	•	•	•	•	•	•
Mammoth (open all year)	•	•	•	•	•	•	•	•	•		•
Old Faithful	•	•	•	•	•	•	•	•	•	•	•
Roosevelt	•	•	•	•	•		•	•	•		•
Tower Fall	•	•	•	•	•	•	•	•	•		•

CAMPGROUNDS AND OTHER FACILITIES

	Auto Service (Emerg.)	Boating	Boat Rental	Camp Sites	Evening Program	Fireplaces	Fishing	Horse Rental	Medical Clinic	Laundry (Coin-Op)	Diesel Fuel	Piped Water	Post Office	Propane Service	Sanitary Facilities	Service Station	Shower (Public)	R V Dump Station	R V Park (Utilities-Fee)	Trailers (No Hookup)
Bridge Bay		•	•	420	•	•	•					•			•			•		•
Canyon Village	•			280	•	•	•	•		•	•	•	•		•	•	•	•		•
Fishing Bridge	•				•	•	•			•	•	•		•	•	•	•	•	•	•
Grant Village	•	•		403	•	•	•			•		•	•	•	•	•	•	•		•
Indian Creek				75	•	•	•					•			•					•
Lake							•		•	•			•							
Lewis Lake		•		85	•	•	•					•			•					•
Madison				292	•	•	•					•			•				•	•
Mammoth				85	•	•	•	•	•		•	•	•		•	•				•
Norris				116	•	•	•					•			•					•
Old Faithful	•				•		•		•		•	•	•	•		•	•			
Pebble Creek				36		•	•					•			•					•
Roosevelt Lodge/ Tower Fall				32	•	•	•	•			•	•			•	•				•
Slough Creek				29		•	•								•					•

OTHER THINGS TO DO

	Bridge Bay	Canyon Village	Fishing Bridge	Grant Village	Lake	Mammoth	Norris	Old Faithful	Roosevelt Lodge/ Tower Fall
Evening Programs	•	•	•	•		•	•	•	•
Scenic Cruises	•								
Stage Coach Rides									•
Bus Tours		•			•	•		•	
Visitor Center		•	•	•		•	•	•	
Conducted Walk		•	•	•		•	•	•	•

REGULATIONS

Regulations are necessary to preserve the Park and to provide for your safety. By observing the regulations (which are enforced by Park rangers), you and those after you will be able to enjoy the Park safely and happily.

The following are some special hazards to watch out for in Yellowstone.

- All Park animals are wild and, if harrassed, potentially dangerous. Don't get close to any animal and watch the large ones from your vehicle only. Use the roadside pullouts for observation so the rest of the traffic can go by.

- In the thermal areas, boiling water may be very close beneath the surface. It's unlawful, unsafe, and possibly destructive to the thermal features to leave the designated pathways.

- The water in Yellowstone's lakes is cold, averaging 4.4°C. (41°F.). Most people could survive for no more than 30 minutes in these waters, therefore only hardsided boats are allowed.

- Yellowstone's streams are big, fast, and cold. Swimming is not advised and caution is urged while fishing or wading.

- Stay on the designated trails while in the canyon areas. The steep slopes often contain loose rocks and soil; thus, climbing here is dangerous. (And unlawful.)

These regulations deserve special attention:

- Permits are required for fishing, boating, and back-country travel.
- Pets must be kept leashed and on roadsides and parking areas only.
- It's unlawful to pick wildflowers, litter, or vandalize any of the Park's features. This includes removing "souvenir" rocks, etc.
- It's against the law to swim or bathe in the thermal features.
- Firearms may never be carried or displayed.
- All wheeled vehicles are restricted to roadways except in designated areas.
- Fires must never be left unattended.

Check with a ranger if you are unsure about any activity. Violators of any of the Park regulations will be taken before a resident U.S. Magistrate who is authorized to assess fines or imprison offenders.

Bison herd

ADMINISTRATION

Yellowstone National Park was established by an Act of Congress and signed by President Ulysses S. Grant on March 1, 1872. The National Park Service was established in 1916. The National Parks are under the jurisdiction of the Secretary of the Interior.

The Park Superintendent is responsible for the overall operation of Yellowstone National Park. He and his staff administer the Park through such divisions as the Ranger Service, Administrative Offices, Concessions Management, Engineering, and Maintenance. The Superintendent formulates Park policies and directs their enforcement. He is charged with the protection and preservation of natural features and wildlife including flora and fauna.

The Ranger Service has two divisions: Law Enforcement and Interpretive.

A Chief Ranger administers the Law Enforcement Division whose duties include, among many, winter patrols to protect the Park; car patrols to regulate traffic; enforce rules and regulations; investigate accidents; man the entrance gates; operate ranger stations; and protect natural features and wildlife.

The Interpretive Division is administered by the Chief Park Naturalist. His division is charged with explaining natural and historical features with visitor centers, guided walks, and evening programs at amphitheaters. The Chief Naturalist administers a library at Headquarters (Mammoth Hot Springs), and issues publications.

The Park Ranger and Park Ranger Naturalist staff is augmented during the summer months by seasonal employees. Many are university or high school teachers. Some are university students. Those in the Interpretive Division are students of sciences such as conservation, botany, geology, biology, and other disciplines dealing with natural resources. Some of the seasonal Naturalists are historians. All are very carefully selected and dedicated. Many of the seasonal staff of both ranger divisions return year after year.

U.S. MAIL SERVICE

The main U.S. Post Office is located at Mammoth Hot Springs and is open all year. The address is: Yellowstone National Park, Wyoming 82190. In the summer, additional post offices are located at Old Faithful, Grant Village, Lake, and Canyon Village.

Do not address mail in care of a Park Entrance. If you have reservations at hotels or lodges, mail may be sent to you in care of them. General Delivery Mail addressed to Yellowstone National Park, Wyoming 82190 must be called for at the Post Office at Mammoth Hot Springs.

MEDICAL SERVICE

West Park Hospital of Cody, Wyoming has its Park headquarters at Lake Hospital. It is completely equipped and staffed to take care of medical emergencies arising during the tourist season.

Staff physicians have ambulance and transportation facilities, and are on call at Mammoth Clinic and Lake Hospital. They will attend patients any place in the Park upon call. Winter address: West Park Hospital, Cody, Wyoming 82414.

Emergency Information

Assistance for any emergency in the Park can be obtained any time by calling Park headquarters (307) 344-7381 or 911.

Medical Assistance

Lake Hospital	Memorial Day - Mid Sept.	(307)	242-7241
Mammoth Clinic	Year around	(307)	344-7965
Old Faithful Clinic	Memorial Day - Early Oct.	(307)	545-7325

CONCESSIONERS

All concessioners conduct their enterprises in Yellowstone National Park under Government franchises and lease land from the Government. Buildings and equipment are owned by Hamilton Stores or the Government. The Government regulates the types of services and prices.

The concessioners are in the Park to serve you. They employ people who are trained to meet Yellowstone visitors and cater to their wants. It is their desire to serve you competently.

Hamilton Stores Inc. operates general stores, tackle shops, and photo shops within Yellowstone Park and offer a wide selection of fine gifts, souvenirs, photo supplies, groceries, fishing/camping equipment, Indian artwork, clothing and food service. The summer address is: Hamilton Stores Inc., P.O. Box 250, West Yellowstone, Montana 59785. The winter address is: Hamilton Stores, Inc., 1709 W. College, Bozeman, MT 59715.

The **Yellowstone Park Division, TW Recreational Services, Inc.** operates hotels, motor inns, restaurants, lodges, cabins, transportation, bus tours, saddle horse trips, stagecoach rides, boating, and fishing guide services.

Reservations and information requests should be directed to Yellowstone Park Division, TW Recreational Services, Inc., Reservations Department, Yellowstone National Park, Wyoming 82190. Year-round phone (307) 344-7901. Requests should include number in party, arrival date, length of stay, type of accommodation and Park location desired, or tour. If prepaid, your check, payable to "Yellowstone Park Division, TW Recreational Services, Inc.," should be sent 14 days in advance of arrival.

Yellowstone Park Service Stations are operated by Hamilton Stores, Inc., and TW Recreational Services, Inc., partners. Stations are located at all areas around the Loop Road except Madison Junction, Norris Junction, Lake and West Thumb.

CHURCH SERVICES

Church services are conducted at all major centers during the summer months, usually late May or early June through August.

Protestant   Latter-day Saints
Roman Catholic   Seventh-day Adventists

Consult schedule posted in visitor centers, Hamilton Stores and Photo Shops, hotels, lodges, cabin offices, and service stations.

Similar church services are held in Grand Teton National Park. Communities adjoining Yellowstone National Park also conduct services; for example, West Yellowstone, Gardiner, and Cooke City, Montana; Cody and Jackson, Wyoming.

RECREATIONAL FACILITIES
General Information

Boating: You can rent rowboats, motorboats, and cruisers at Bridge Bay on Yellowstone Lake. There are launching facilities for small private boats, as well. Some lakes, and parts of Yellowstone Lake, are reserved for hand-propelled craft only. Some areas have speed restrictions (see map).

Camping: Limited camping is available all year; however, the majority of campgrounds are open only from mid-June to mid-September. The major campgrounds are normally filled by noon during the summer. Camping or overnight stopping is permitted only in designated campgrounds. When Park campgrounds are full, camping visitors, including persons with self-contained recreational vehicles, must find facilities outside the Park. Your stay in the Park as a camper is limited to 14 days during the summer and to a total of 30 days per year. Fishing Bridge and Canyon are restricted to hard-sided vehicles. Two campgrounds are available for organized groups and should be reserved by contacting the chief park ranger's office.

Aspen Grove Along the Lamar River

Hiking: There are over 1,200 miles of trails that reach all parts of the Park. Many are pleasant one-or-two-hour walks, or half-day hikes. You'll find nature walks, footpaths that guide you through geyser basins, and more rigorous trails to observation points. Most are marked with directional signs giving destinations and distances. You can purchase good topographic maps at any Hamilton Store. Always check trail conditions with a ranger before setting out on a long hike.

Horseback Riding: See Yellowstone from on top of a horse! Trail horses can be rented for one or two hours at Canyon, Mammoth, or Tower-Roosevelt. Private outfitters outside the park are available and arrangements can be made for guided pack trips into the park.

Stagecoach Rides: Bounce across Pleasant Valley in a colorful, sturdy, Concord stagecoach for a thrilling, historic look at Yellowstone. Stages depart hourly from the corral at Roosevelt Lodge, near Tower Junction.

Tours

By Boat: 40-passenger excursion boats leave Bridge Bay Marina several times daily. Special twilight cruises embark each evening. You'll see ducks, geese, pelicans, and maybe even browsing elk and moose along the shoreline.

By Bus: Your driver will stop at major attractions along the way and give you plenty of time for taking pictures. Tour brochures are available at Yellowstone Park Division, TW Recreation Services, Inc. facilities.

The following sections give you more detailed information on camping, fishing and boating, hiking (including back-country), and picnic facilities.

Stagecoach Ride

Boats

CAMPGROUND LISTING

Tents and trailers are permitted in all of the campgrounds listed below except Canyon and Fishing Bridge Campgrounds which are restricted to hard-sided camp units. There are no electrical or plumbing hookups, nor are shower facilities available. These campgrounds are unreserved. Sites are available on a first-come, first-served basis. A fee is charged.

Name and Location	Approx. Elev.	No. Camp Sites	Approximate Seasons	Piped Water	Flush Toilet
*Bridge Bay 3 mi. S. of Lake	7800	420	5/25-9/15	Yes	Yes
Canyon **1/4 mi. E. of Canyon Junction	8000	280	6/5-9/10	Yes	Yes
**Grant Village 2 mi. S. West Thumb Junction	7800	403	6/20-10/15	Yes	Yes
Indian Creek 7½ mi. S. Mammoth	7300	75	6/5-9/15	Yes	No
*Lewis Lake 10 mi. S. West Thumb	7800	85	6/15-10/31	Yes	No
Madison 1/4 mi. W. of Madison Junction	6800	292	5/1-10/31	Yes	Yes
**Mammoth 1/2 mi. N. of Mammoth Junction	6000	85	All Year	Yes	Yes
Norris 1/2 mi. N. of Norris Junction	7500	116	5/15-9/30	Yes	Yes
Pebble Creek 7 mi. SE Northeast Entrance	6900	36	6/15-9/10	Yes	No
Slough Creek 10 mi. E. Tower Fall Junction	6250	29	5/25-10/31	Yes	No
Tower Fall 3 mi. E. of Tower Junction	6600	32	5/31-9/15	Yes	No

*Boat launching facilities near these campgrounds.
**Concessioner-operated shower and laundry facilities located nearby development.

GENERAL RULES AND REGULATIONS
GOVERNING CAMPGROUND USE

CAMPING LIMITATIONS   June 16 to August 25 — 14 days, in a single period or 30 days per season.

Labor Day to June 26 — 30 days.

CAMPING AND SANITATION   Campers must keep their campsites clean. Combustible rubbish should be burned in campfires, and all other garbage refuse placed in provided receptacles.

The drainage or dumping of refuse from any trailer or pickup camper, except in places or receptacles provided for such purpose, is prohibited. All campers should carry their waste water to the nearest rest-room for disposal.

The cleaning of fish, or the washing of clothing, at campground hydrants, is prohibited.

Quiet is maintained between the hours of 8:00 pm and 8:00 am.

Campers must not leave their camps unattended for more than 24 hours without special permission of a Park ranger.

A commercial trailer park with 358 sites at Fishing Bridge, which operates from approximately Memorial Day to September 10, provides water, sewer, and power hookups at a nominal rate. Self-service laundry facilities, showers, and hair dryers are also available for a nominal charge. Length of stay for any one season is a total of 14 days. Reservations may be made by writing to Fishing Bridge Trailer Village, Yellowstone National Park, Wyoming 82190.

FOOD STORAGE SUGGESTIONS FOR CAMPERS

Any food or food container that smells or is left on tables or in open boxes—or *any* garbage, for that matter—is a definite invitation to bears and is in violation of Park Service regulations. Generally, campers who keep a clean camp are less likely to be bothered by bears.

1. Food should not be stored on a table or in your tent.
2. Seal surplus food in clean wrapping material or in airtight containers.
3. Keep your food as cool as possible.
4. Your car trunk is one of the best food storage places.
5. Report all bear damage and injuries to a Park ranger.

FIRES

In public campgrounds, build fires only in the regular fireplaces. Fires shall be completely extinguished when the campsite is left unattended. Fire permits are required for fires in back-country and wilderness locations. Fireworks and firecrackers are prohibited.

PETS

All pets must be on a leash or otherwise under restrictive control at all times. Pets are not allowed in the back country on the trails and boardwalks in thermal areas.

LOST ARTICLES

Persons finding lost articles should deposit them at the nearest ranger station, leaving their own names and addresses. Articles not claimed by the owner within 60 days shall be returned to the finder.

FISHING AND BOATING

You are permitted to fish in Yellowstone National Park, but the regulations have been designed to give the grizzly bear, otter, osprey, and other animals first chance at catching a fish. A free permit is required because regulations vary widely throughout the Park. Most streams and some lakes are closed to all boats while others are zoned for use only with canoes and rowboats. In certain areas, zoning is designed to protect wildlife that would otherwise be driven from their native haunts. It is the policy of the National Park Service to maintain the fish to form continuous breeding populations.

The only game fish native to Yellowstone are the cutthroat or black spotted trout (*salmo clarki*) and the mountain whitefish (*prosopium williamsoni*). Other game fish include: brook trout (*salvelinus fontinalis*), rainbow trout (*salmo gairdneri*), brown trout also called loch leven (*salmo trutta*), grayling (*thymallus arcticus*), and mackinaw (*salvelinus namaycush*).

Cutthroat trout are scattered throughout the lakes and streams in the Park, but are common in Yellowstone Lake, streams that lead into it, and the Yellowstone River.

Grayling inhabit the Grayling Lakes (Wolf Lake and Grebe Lake) between Norris and Canyon. Mackinaw prefer the cold deep waters of Lewis Lake and Shoshone Lake. Brook trout are generally in the streams in the northeast and western sections of the Park. Brown trout find the Firehole and Madison Rivers as favorite habitats.

Complete fishing tackle can be rented or purchased at the marinas on Yellowstone Lake and tackle is available at all Hamilton Stores. Experienced guides and rental boats are available at the docks. Saddle horses can be rented for trips to more remote lakes and streams.

HIKING
Back-country trails on foot or in the saddle

In Yellowstone's "back-country," wildlife remains undisturbed in superb mountain scenery. The trails lead you to many "away-from-the-road" attractions and will allow you to discover Yellowstone in an unforgettable way that's impossible if you choose to stay close to your car.

A free back-country use and fire permit is required; and, if you plan to camp in the back-country, you must reserve a campsite. Reservations must be made in person no more than 48 hours prior to your departure time and can be made at all ranger stations and some visitor centers.

The National Park Service has written a booklet called "Beyond Road's End" which outlines the rules and regulations for Yellowstone's back-country and provides useful hints for hikers and riders. Be sure to pick up a copy before you start your adventure.

HORSE AND FOOT TRAILS

Explore America's wilderness heritage the way the first explorers did— on foot or on horseback. You'll discover the same unspoiled, unchanged beauty and solitude. And, there's enough wide open spaces in the list below for even the hardiest adventurer! There are 1200 miles of trails and 85 trailheads.

SOME TRAILS	Distance
Thunderer Cutoff to Cache Creek Cabin	7.5
Pebble Creek to Warm Creek	12.0
Cache Creek to Republic Pass	17.0
Amethyst Mountain to Lamar	16.0
Blacktail Creek to Yellowstone River	5.0
Mammoth to Sportsman's Lake and Gallatin	24.0
Rescue Creek to Blacktail Creek	0.7
Gallatin to Bighorn Peak and Shelf Lake	10.0
Specimen Creek to Crescent Lake and High Lake	10.0
Gallatin to Fawn Pass and Mammoth	25.0
Gallatin to Bighorn Pass and Indian Creek	25.0
Madison Ford to West Boundary	16.0
Winter Creek to West Boundary	24.0
Canyon to Cascade Lake, Grebe Lake and Norris	12.0
Otter Creek to Nez Perce	20.0
Upper Falls to Fern Lake and Pelican Creek	29.0
Indian Pond to Cold Creek	19.0

These trails are plainly marked by National Park Service Signs along the park roads.

PICNIC FACILITIES

Camping is not allowed in the picnic areas. There are grills at Bridge Bay, Grant Village and Lava Creek. Most of the areas are supplied with pit toilets. Drinking water is generally not available at the picnic areas.

Name	Location	Sites
Antelope Creek	Between Tower Fall and Canyon	1
Apollinaris Springs	Between Mammoth and Norris Junction	5
Beaver Pond	Between Mammoth and Norris Junction	12
Bridge Bay	At Bridge Bay Marina Area	38
Buffalo Ford	Between Canyon Village and Lake Junction	6
Cascade Meadows	Between Canyon and Tower Fall	15
De Lacy Creek	Between West Thumb and Old Faithful	9
Divide	Between Old Faithful and West Thumb	8
Dunraven Pass	Between Tower Fall and Canyon Village	10
Feather Lake	On Fountain Freight Road Between Madison Junction and Old Faithful	6
Firehole	Between Madison Junction and Old Faithful	12
Frank Island	Frank Island, Lake Yellowstone	8
Gibbon Falls	Between Norris Junction and Madison Junction	18
Gibbon Meadows	Between Norris Junction and Madison Junction	9
Gibbon River (Norris)	Between Norris Junction and Canyon Village	3
Goose Lake	On Fountain Freight Road Between Madison Junction and Old Faithful	6

Grant Village	At Grant Village Near Marina	24
Gull Point	Between Lake Junction and West Thumb	9
Hayden Valley	Between Canyon and Lake	8
Hellroaring	Between Mammoth and Tower Junction	4
Lake Eleanor	Between Fishing Bridge and East Entrance	3
Lamar	Between Tower Junction and North East Entrance	4
Lava Creek	Between Mammoth and Tower Fall	10
Le Hardy Rapids	Between Lake and Canyon	5
Lone Star	Between Old Faithful and West Thumb	4
Madison Junction	Madison Junction, Near Visitor Center	14
Madison River	Between Madison Junction and West Entrance	4
Mary Bay	Between Fishing Bridge and East Entrance	1
Morning Glory	Between Old Faithful and Madison Junction	6
Nez Perce	Between Old Faithful and Madison Junction	6
Norris Geyser Basin	At Norris Geyser Basin Parking Area	
Old Dunraven Road	Between Canyon and Tower Fall	13
Petrified Tree	Between Mammoth and Tower Junction	2
Pumice Point	Between Lake Junction and West Thumb	9
Sand Bar Reef	Between Bridge Bay and West Thumb	3
Sand Point	Between Lake Junction and West Thumb	19
Scenic Overlook	Between Bridge Bay and West Thumb	8
Sedge Bay	Between Fishing Bridge and East Entrance	3
Sheepeater Cliff	Between Mammoth and Norris Junction	3
Spring Creek	Between Old Faithful and West Thumb	10
Steamboat Point	Between Fishing Bridge and East Entrance	9
Sylvan Lake	Between Fishing Bridge and East Entrance	9
Tuff Cliff	Between Norris Junction and Madison Junction	4
Virginia Cascades	Between Norris Junction and Canyon Village	3
Virginia Meadows	Between Norris Junction and Canyon	4
Warm Creek	Between Lamar and North East Entrance	1
Whisky Flats	Between Old Faithful and Madison Junction	15
Yellowstone River	Between Canyon Village and Lake Junction	10
Yellowstone River Bridge	Between Tower Junction and Lamar	6

THE FOUR SEASONS OF YELLOWSTONE

SPRING

Spring is a magnificent time to visit Yellowstone, You'll witness the magic of nature's renewal as new life is evidenced in budding wildflowers and in young animals who test their wobbly legs. Roaring waterfalls carry away the melting winter snow and awakening bears welcome the nourishment they find in the new rich green vegetation. Resident bird species and springtime visitors on their flight back north feed in the Park's many lakes and marshes. The mornings are brisk, the nights are cold, and the days are sunny in this the first season of Yellowstone's year.

SUMMER

Yellowstone's busiest season is filled with activities ranging from fishing and hiking to evening campfire programs and stagecoach rides. Geysers erupt and thermal pools hiss and boil over. The days are warm; the evenings, cool. Although the season is busy, there is still time for relaxation and contemplation within the beautiful boundaries of the Park.

AUTUMN

The pace slows during Yellowstone's third season. The days are full of brilliant reds, yellows, and golds in trees that are preparing for the winter snow. The cooler weather brings the wildlife back down from the high plateaus to graze and mate. Fishing, horseback riding, and hiking are still popular activities during the resplendent Yellowstone Indian Summer.

WINTER

The robust Yellowstone winter is sharp and cold and spectacular with beauty. The land is blanketed with snow and loosely covered with a quilt of vapor clouds rising from the thermal areas. The Park can be toured by snowshoe, cross-country ski, snowmobile, or snow coach. (The Old Faithful, Mammoth and West Yellowstone areas supply snowshoe and ski lessons, equipment rental, and tours.)

You can explore the "White Face of Yellowstone" in comfortable 10-passenger over-the-snow vehicles that can be boarded at the West, North and South entrances. Private snowmobilers and back-country skiers and snowshoers must observe Park regulations, so be sure to contact Park rangers before leaving.

Meals and overnight rooms are available from late December through mid-March at the Old Faithful Snow Lodge, and Mammoth Hot Springs Hotel. Information and reservations on winter activities and lodging may be obtained by writing to Yellowstone National Park, Wyoming 82190. Reservations are especially advisable during the holidays. Also open during this period are Hamilton Stores at Mammoth carrying a full line of general merchandise and food services.

CHART OF INTERESTING ELEVATIONS
ENTRANCE GATES

North.. 5,314 feet
West... 6,667 feet
South.. 6,886 feet
East... 6,951 feet
Northeast.................................... 7,365 feet

VILLAGES AND JUNCTIONS

Mammoth Hot Springs.......................... 6,239 feet
Norris Junction.............................. 7,484 feet
Madison Junction............................. 6,806 feet
Old Faithful Area............................ 7,365 feet
West Thumb Area.............................. 7,733 feet
Lake Junction................................ 7,784 feet
Canyon Village............................... 7,734 feet
Tower Junction............................... 6,270 feet
Grant Village................................ 7,733 feet

CONTINENTAL DIVIDES

Between Old Faithful and West Thumb:
   Isa Lake at Craig Pass.................... 8,262 feet
   Herron and DeLacy Creek drainage,
      west of Yellowstone Lake............. 8,391 feet
Between West Thumb and South Entrance
   approximately 4 miles from West Thumb.... 7,988 feet
Yellowstone Lake.............................. 7,731 feet

PRIMARY FIRE LOOKOUTS

Mt. Washburn, between Canyon and Tower Junction ......10,234 feet
Mt. Holmes, Northeast........................ 10,336 feet
Mt. Sheridan, South near Heart Lake.......... 10,308 feet

HIGHEST MOUNTAIN IN
YELLOWSTONE NATIONAL PARK

Eagle Peak — Southeast Boundary.............. 11,358 feet

LOWEST ELEVATION

Yellowstone River near North Boundary, approximately.... 5,000 feet

PASSES

Kingman Pass, between Mammoth Hot Springs
   and Norris Junction.................... 7,250 feet
Craig Pass, between Old Faithful and West Thumb........ 8,262 feet
Sylvan Pass, between Lake Junction and East Entrance.... 8,530 feet
Dunraven Pass, between Canyon Junction and Tower Fall.. 8,859 feet

GEYSERS — AN EXPLANATION

What is the explanation for geyser eruptions? Years of scientific research have helped to solve some of the unknown facts. Some factors still remain unknown. The U.S. Geological Survey explains the intricacies of a typical geyser eruption as follows:

The tube leading up to the surface vent on the cone before you has been measured to a depth of 70 feet. Beyond that, the descent becomes too crooked to follow with a weighted rope. Apparently it twists downward hundreds of feet more and becomes lost in a maze of subterranean tubes, pipes, and chambers. Although down there the temperature is well above boiling, the water does not boil due to the pressure from the weight of the overlying water higher in the system. Roughly the same sort of thing happens in a pressure cooker on the kitchen stove. Put an open pot of water on the burner and before long, boiling begins with the liquid, water, changing into gas, steam, which disappears into the air of the kitchen. But clamp a tight lid over the pot and the steam cannot escape. Since the confined space can only hold so much, soon no more water can turn into steam. The boiling stops even though the water gets hotter and hotter. The steam gets hotter, too, and if there were not a safety valve on the pressure cooker, the pot would explode. Now, the confining water in the geyser's plumbing system is not as rigid as the top of a pressure cooker. When the water deep in the system gets hot enough, some steam does form. This expanding steam lifts the overlying water in the pipe leading to the surface. Before the main eruption, you will see some water come splashing out of Old Faithful. Usually most of this ejected water will fall back in the vent and the volume of water in the system will not be greatly changed. These false starts may occur a number of times but, eventually, enough water will be thrown out to reduce the weight of water in the vent pipe. The eruption is now triggered. With the confining pressure slightly released, the overheated water down below flashes into steam, lifts more water out of the top, and generates more steam, and so on in a rapidly accelerating steam explosion. The explosion violently blasts the hot boiling mixture of water and steam high into the air through the nozzle-like vent. The eruption is on!

GEYSERS AT UPPER GEYSER BASIN

Name	Interval	Height	Duration
Anemone Geyser	7-13 minutes	4-7 feet	30-60 seconds
Artemisia Geyser	8-½-16 hours	15-35 feet	5-25 minutes
Atomizer Geyser	Cycl., 1 or more daily	10-35 feet	1-10 minutes
Beach Spring	Cyclic	1-3 feet	Seconds

Name	Interval	Height	Duration
Beehive Geyser	1-6 days*	100-180 feet	4-8 minutes
Big Cub Geyser	Rare	30-40 feet	3-8 minutes
Bijou Geyser	Almost steady	3-30 feet	Hours to days
Black Pearl Geyser	Almost steady*	4-8 feet	Seconds
Bulger Geyser	Cyclic	2-8 feet	1-20 minutes
Cascade Geyser	Rare	15-30 feet	1-4 minutes
Castle Geyser	7-12 hours	63-100 feet	15-20 minutes
Catfish Geyser	Cyclic*	3-75 feet	2-20 minutes
Cauliflower Geyser	50-90 minutes	1 foot	2-3 minutes
Chinaman Spring	Rare	20-40 feet	2 minutes
Churn Geyser	Infrequent	1 foot	2-3 minutes
Cliff Geyser	Hours to days*	20-35 feet	2-3 hours
Comet Geyser	Almost steady	2-6 feet	Almost steady
Daisy Geyser	45 min. to 4 hours*	75-100 feet	3-1/2-5 minutes
Dragon Spring	Dormant	Boil	Few minutes
Echinus Geyser	45 to 60 minutes	75 feet	5 to 14 minutes
Economic Geyser	Variable	8-30 feet	Seconds
Fan Geyser	Rare	80-125 feet	60-90 minutes
Giant Geyser	Rare	120-225 feet	90-115 minutes
Giantess Geyser	Rare	75-200 feet	12-43 hours
Grand Geyser	6-15 hours	140-200 feet	9-16 minutes
Green Spring	Rare, cyclic	6-25 feet	4 min. to hours
Grotto Geyser	Cyclic, 1-12 hours	8-40 feet	1-8 hours
Grotto Fountain Geyser	Cyclic	20-50 feet	10-20 minutes
Infant Geyser	Variable	1-1/2-3 feet	Seconds
Jewel Geyser	5-10 minutes	5-22 feet	45-90 seconds
Link Geyser	1-4 hours	3-75 feet	1-15 minutes
Lion Geyser	Cyclic,1/2-3 days*	50-60 feet	2-6 minutes
Lioness Geyser	Dormant	20-50 feet	2-1/2-10 minutes
Little Brother Geyser	5-20 minutes*	2-15 feet	1/2-6 minutes
Little Cub Geyser	4 min.-4 hours	1-10 feet	1-15 minutes
Mastiff Geyser	Rare	4-100 feet	Variable
Midget Geyser	50-60 minutes	3-4 feet	5-7 minutes
Mortar Geyser	2-7 days	7-25 feet	6-15 minutes
Oblong Geyser	3-18 hours	20-40 feet	6-8 minutes
Old Faithful Geyser	70-80 minutes	106-184 feet	1-1/2-5-1/2 minutes
Plume Geyser	22-70 minutes	20-35 feet	1-2 minutes
Pump Geyser	Almost steady	1-3 feet	Almost steady
Rainbow Pool	Rare	15-100 feet	5-10 minutes
Riverside Geyser	5-9 hours	75-80 feet	16-23 minutes
Rocket Geyser	Cyclic, 1-12 hours	5-40 feet	2-5 minutes

Name	Interval	Height	Duration
Round Geyser	2-15 hours*	40-115 feet	½-1-½ minutes
Sapphire Pool	Dormant	4-150 feet	2-8 minutes
Sawmill Geyser	1-6 hours	17-34 feet	1-4 hours
Seismic Geyser	Rare	6-50 feet	15-30 minutes
Sentinel Geyser	Rare	20-30 feet	Unrecorded
Solitary Geyser	2-6 minutes	5-12 feet	1-3 minutes
Spa Geyser	Rare	10-50 feet	30-90 minutes
Spanker	Steady	4-6 feet	Steady
Spasmodic Geyser	Daily	3-20 feet	20-40 minutes
Splendid Geyser	Dormant	100-180 feet	2-10 minutes
Sponge Geyser	1 minute*	6-12 inches	Seconds
Spouter Geyser	Almost steady	4-7 feet	Almost steady
Sprinkler Geyser	Frequent	4-6 feet	15-20 minutes
Tardy Geyser	Minutes to hours	3-25 feet	Minutes to hours
Three Sisters Springs	35-50 minutes	15-30 feet	2-3 minutes
Triplet Geysers	1-2 hours	20-25 feet	2-3 minutes
Turban Geyser	15-25 minutes	4-10 feet	4-60 minutes
Vault Geyser	Cyclic, 45-70 min.*	2-15 feet	3-20 minutes
Whistle Geyser	Rare	35-40 feet	2-3 hours
White Geyser	1-20 minutes*	7-45 feet	20-180 seconds

*Sometimes dormant for long periods.

Hamilton General Store

Silex Spring, Lower Geyser Basin

Old Faithful Inn

FACTS ABOUT OLD FAITHFUL GEYSER

The following facts and theories about Old Faithful were obtained from the Office of the Chief Park Naturalist in Yellowstone:

1. Old Faithful was undoubtedly known to trappers from 1833 on, but was not named or fully described until the Washburn-Langford-Doane expedition of 1870.

2. It plays as regularly and as high now as it did when they first saw it.

3. During the 1979 season, the 3521 timed intervals between eruptions indicated that the average interval was 72.5 minutes. The shortest interval between eruptions was 36 minutes, and the longest interval was 102 minutes. Of the more than 65,000 observed and recorded eruptions in the last 110 years, Old Faithful's average interval has *always* been between 60 and 67 minutes. In this same period of time, the minimum interval recorded was 33 minutes, and the maximum was 102 minutes.

4. The duration of Old Faithful's eruptions varies from 1½ to 5½ minutes.

5. The amount of water thrown out of the geyser during the eruption was carefully estimated by Dr. Eugene Robertson of the U.S. Geological Survey. It was determined that from 5,000 to 7,500 gallons of water were ejected. Most of the water thrown out of Old Faithful runs into the Firehole River.

6. Geyser tubes or wells are not uniform in shape. They are usually crooked or constricted in many places. Attempts to plumb the depth of Old Faithful indicate that there is a constriction at about 70 feet. It is not known how much deeper the geyser tube goes.

7. The tremendous amounts of water erupted from such geysers as Old Faithful, Giant, Giantess, Grand, Great Fountain, and other major geysers indicate that large volumes of water move rapidly through the geyser's plumbing during an eruption. Geologists believe that one or more porous, permeable beds of rock, called aquifers, are the reservoirs that supply the water for an eruption.

8. It has been estimated that almost all of the water in geysers and hot springs has its origin as surface water from rain and snow. The water is returned to the surface by steam pressure after being heated in the geyser's subterranean plumbing system. The remainder of the water has its origin in condensed steam from the hot gases rising from magma (molten rock) at considerable depth.

9. Theory suggests that magma is the source of heat for geysers and hot springs. The heat is transmitted through solid rock to water

which has seeped to depths perhaps 10,000 feet below the surface. The very hot water then rises in the plumbing system of a geyser, heating rocks and water that it meets along the way. The amount of heat is suggested by the fact that superheated water flows into a number of hot springs. During an eruption of Old Faithful its water temperature at the vent is approximately 204 degrees Farenheit.

10. The existence of a geyser depends upon:
    a. An adequate supply of water.
    b. A source of heat.
    c. A plumbing system—a series of fissures and fractures that reach deep into the earth.
    d. A rock formation that is sufficiently strong to maintain the plumbing system against the pressure of steam explosions.

ALGAE

The algae (singular, alga) are referred to frequently in describing the color in many hot springs and numerous run-off channels. Algae are structurally simple organisms classified as plants. They are listed in five major groups: *Myxophyta, Chlorophyta, Chrysophyta, Pharophyta,* and *Rhyodphyta.* The latter two groups are almost all macroscopic and marine.

Most algae are aquatic, but some are found on soil and other plants. Algae do not possess roots, stems, or leaves. Some of these primitive plants are microscopic while others are macroscopic. Common forms are observed in ponds and lakes as "pond scum" or "green scum." Among these are spirogyra and oscillatoria. Ocean forms such as "giant sea weeds" may be more than a hundred feet long. Kelp and Sargassum are typical ocean forms.

Many Yellowstone visitors are surprised to learn that certain algae and other organisms can live and grow in hot springs! In a very general way, in run-off channels from hot springs, you can see that the hotter the water is, the lighter the colors (cream to yellow); and the cooler the water is, the darker the colors (green).

BACTERIA

Bacteria occur almost everywhere. They are distributed in the air, soil, and water. They are classified as simple organisms belonging to a group known as *Protists* (a separate kingdom which includes organisms not distinctly plant or animal). Some bacteria are larger than others, but all are microscopic. The bacteria are of special interest in Yellowstone because they, too, are found in hot springs. In fact, some bacteria live and grow essentially at the boiling point of water. However, according to Dr. Thomas D. Brock, Professor of Microbiology at Indiana University, "The upper temperature for life as we know it has not yet been defined . . . [but] there seems to be no reason why bacteria could not live in nature at any temperature where there is liquid water." (From "Life at High Temperatures" reprinted from *Science,* Nov. 24, 1967.)

LICHEN

Lichens are two different kinds of plants living in very close association. One is a producer, an alga, capturing the energy of sunlight and making food by photosynthesis. The other is a fungus (pl., fungi). The fungus is a consumer that lives as a parasite on the producer. The fungus provides support and absorbs water; the alga carries on photosynthesis and contributes food. Both organisms benefit from the association. Such a relationship is called mutualism.

Lichen are among the most widely distributed living forms. In Yellowstone, they are commonly found on rocks and the bark of trees. Lichens possess no roots, stems, or leaves. The colors vary in hues of gray-black, dull gray-green, red-yellow, yellow, and orange.

MISTLETOE — Family Loranthaceae
(Arcenthobium americanum)

The above-named mistletoe is parasitic on lodgepole pine. It occurs on the twigs and branches of pine as a yellowish-green much-branched plant. These parasites do contain chlorophyll, but apparently need cetain carbohydrates, minerals, vitamins, and enzymes which they obtain from their host. The tiny leaves are reduced to leathery scales. The minute flowers are dioecious (bearing pistils and stamens on different plants). A strong lens is needed to see the flowers. Seeds are borne singly in berry-like structures that are equipped with an explosive seed-dispersal mechanism. At maturity, the elastic outer case of the berry, which is filled to capacity with water, breaks from its base, contracts violently, and flings the seed into the air with a force that carries it up to 33 feet away. Winds also aid to carry the seeds. In some recorded instances, they have been blown as far away as a quarter of a mile. Seeds that settle on the lodgepole pine stems may germinate and send absorbing strands into the bark and start new plants. Several years go by before the first shoots are produced. The mistletow frequently produces what is referred to as "witches brooms" where the parasites are especially numerous. Another common result is the swelling of the tree's limbs.

Tower Fall Gorge

GEOLOGY

You don't have to be a geologist to appreciate Yellowstone's great thermal areas, mountains, rivers, waterfalls, canyons, lakes, and petrified trees. A brief explanation of some aspects of the geological processes is presented here for those of you who are curious about "how these things came to be."

A half-billion years ago, Yellowstone was a part of a great barren, desolate plain that covered most of North America. There was no life on the bleak landscape.

Then, for hundreds of millions of years, the oceans from the Arctic and the Pacific inundated the plain. There were many periods of flooding and withdrawal. Tiny calcareous-shelled marine animals lived in the ocean water. When the animals died, the shells fell to the ocean floor. Layer upon layer of shells became impacted in the sediments to form limestone. The fossils of the shelled animals formed in the sediments.

The intervals between invasions of the seas brought climatic changes which produced vegetation. Out of the sea came ancestors of our land animals. The first animals lived in the sea and gradually adapted to live partly on land and to feed on vegetation. Thousands of years were required for the transition from water forms to land dwellers. Dinosaurs and their relatives found marshlands where vegetation flourished. When other seas flooded the area and climatic conditions altered, the food for dinosaurs was destroyed. The dinosaurs became extinct. In time, warm-blooded mammals came upon the scene.

Distant volcanoes caused the earth to heave and buckle as a prelude to volcanism. The sedimentary deposits on the surface where the seas had withdrawn were uplifted to where they can be observed on the Gallatin Mountains and the Beartooth Mountain Range.

The mountains altered the topography. Wind and water erosion began their relentless attack on the mountains. The rivers carried abrasive rock particles which aided in carving out valleys. Sand, gravel, and clay were deposited in the valleys and surrounding terrain. When climatic conditions were favorable, vegetation flourished.

Centuries passed and volcanism shook the earth. Fragmental rock and ash were thrown out over the land over which lava (molten rocks) flowed. The rhyolite so generously spread over Yellowstone at places 59 miles wide and 2,000 feet deep became the dominant rock where the lava cooled.

Obsidian Cliff, the mountain of glass seen between Mammoth and Norris, was a lava flow. Its chemical composition is the same as rhyolite, but it cooled much more quickly to produce the black, glassy appearance. The lava congealed on top of the cliff to form a porous rock called pumice.

On the canyon walls at Tower Fall and at Sheepeater Cliff, another lava flow cooled to form pentagonal rock structures that look like a stockade. This rock is called basalt. Two distinct basalt flows are visible and, below them, are stream gravels resting on volcanic breccia.

The most recent lava flows occurred 70,000 to 80,000 years ago on Pitchstone Plateau in the southwest corner of Yellowstone.

It was during intervals between volcanism that climatic changes occurred which proved favorable for trees to grow. The petrified stumps of 9 to 12 distinct layers of buried forests, one on top of the other, have since been exposed by erosion. This can only mean that after each forest had grown to maturity and was buried by volcanic debris, there were periods without further volcanic activity. These periods were long enough to allow soil to develop and new forests to grow on top of the debris, only to be buried under the next outburst of volcanic debris. These alternations of volcanic activity and quiet periods of forest growth were repeated at least 27 times during the many thousands of years it took for the whole thickness of almost 1,200 feet of volcanic materials to accumulate.

Methods used to calculate age in millions used by scientists are based on the presence of radioactive chemical elements in the rocks and the rate at which they break down to form other elements at a constant rate. Uranium breaks down to form lead at a constant rate, potassium breaks down to form argon, rubidium breaks down to form strontium. By selecting rocks from various geological periods and then measuring the ratio between the elements in pairs, it has been possible to approximate the ages of rocks in years.

Petrifaction occurs when minerals in solution (probably very hot water) fill in the cavities within the empty cells of wood. The cellular walls are surrounded. The absorbed mineral water contained silica in solution and iron, and other minerals provided the color. The state of petrifaction is so perfect that identification with a microscope is possible.

The fossil leaves, needles, and twigs are impressions or compressions in some of the rocks.

The kind of tree and plants that made up the petrified forests were ones that had an annual rainfall of between 50 to 60 inches. The elevation probably did not exceed 3,000 feet and the terrain was hilly in some areas and, in others, low broad valleys. It was a warm-temperature to subtropical climate.

The petrified wood and the fossil leaves identified the following plants: Walnuts, sycamores, redwoods (*Sequoia*), maples, hickories, elms, oaks, chestnuts, laurels, figs, and ferns. Over a hundred different species have been identified.

The petrified trees of Yellowstone are unique. Many are standing upright where they grew. They cover a larger area (40 square miles) than any other region of petrified forests.

What does the future hold for Yellowstone? The lakes, rivers, canyons, mountains, and thermal features are but a temporary stage if one reckons in terms of millions of years. Nature is dynamic, not static. Who can predict with surety what the next million years will bring? Will the geysers and other thermal features disappear? Will the rock barrier at the Upper Falls finally be dislodged by the erosive power of the Yellowstone River and, if so, will Yellowstone Lake be drained? Will volcanism, with spewing ash and fragmental rock, mantle the present Yellowstone? Will lava flows pour out over the landscape? And will glacial rivers of ice carry boulders and gravel to distant places in the Park? Will earthquakes cause faults and fractures and landslides such as occurred in 1959?

Only time will answer the above questions.

SOME YELLOWSTONE ANIMALS

Yellowstone National Park is a great wildlife sanctuary where animals live and reproduce in a natural environment. They are protected and are free to roam at will. Listed and briefly described are a few of the species found in the Park. You will surely see some of them during your visit. Remember, for your safety, observe the Park regulations and don't feed, tease, or molest any of the animals. Though they may appear tame, they are unpredictable and potentially dangerous.

During the summer, early morning and late evening are the best time to see the animals. The animals are also in greater evidence during the early (May-mid-June) and late (mid-Sept.-Oct.) seasons when Park traffic is reduced.

On the following pages, you'll meet some of the better-known animals that reside in the Park, plus some suggested seasons and locations for sighting them, and a host of other informational tidbits about our wonderful wildlife neighbors.

Bison

Bison & Calf

Black Bear

Black Bear — *Ursus americanus.*

Black bears have color phases ranging from black to brown and cinnamon. They have a brownish muzzle. Mature bears weigh from 250-350 lbs. They have sharp curved claws which enable adults and cubs to climb trees with great agility.

Bears are omnivorous and eat a great variety of foods in their natural environment. They eat grass, berries, fruits, nuts, insects, fish and carrion.

During autumn or early winter the bears become fat and sleek. They seek a den or cave where they hibernate until spring. There is controversy as to whether or not this winter sleep is true hibernation. Cubs, one to four, are born in January or February and are naked and helpless at birth. The cubs weigh 9-12 ozs. when born. The cubs remain with their mother all summer and return to hibernate with her that autumn. When mating season approaches during the following summer, the cubs are dismissed by their mother and are on their own. Black bears have a family once in two years.

Bears have poor vision, but that is compensated for by an excellent sense of hearing and smell.

Grizzly Mother and Cubs

Grizzly Bear — *Ursus horribilis*

Yellowstone is one of the few remaining strongholds of the grizzly in the contiguous United States. Threatened with extinction, this large bear is most common in the wilderness sections of the Park.

Grizzly bears, at maturity, weigh between 400-600 lbs. They, like the black bear, have color phases from tan to black but with a gray tinge. The grizzly has a distinctive hump on the shoulders. The longest hairs on the hump are often silver-tipped. The face is dished or concave.

Grizzly bears are omnivorous, eating great varieties of plant and animal foods. The diet includes insects, rodents, fruits, berries, fish and other animals that have died or that they have killed.

The claws are sometimes four inches long and are not curved in the manner of black bears. The claws on the front feet are used for digging rodents and tearing decayed logs apart in search of ants or other insects. Adult grizzlies do not climb trees.

Grizzly bears like to roam over large areas. They have well established trails.

Like the black bears, grizzlies seek a den or cave for winter sleep from November to March. Female grizzlies usually have one family every two years. The cubs, usually twins, weigh 16 ozs. at birth.

Elk

Elk (Wapiti) — *Cervus elaphus*

Yellowstone has the largest concentration of Elk to be found anywhere in the world. Elk are members of the deer family. They are larger than deer. Mature bulls weigh from 700-900 lbs. Bulls produce heavy spreading antlers which are shed annually in late winter or early spring. The females do not grow antlers and are smaller than the bulls.

Rutting season occurs in autumn. At this time, the bulls bugle with a low pitched note that ends with a scream and then short grunts.

The calves are born in June. A cow has one or two calves with spots, which, scattered over the body, serve as a camouflage that blends with the meadow vegetation.

The elk in summer are a yellowish red brown and gray brown in winter. They have a white rump patch and a short white tail. During the summer months, elk graze along rivers and streams in the meadows in the central plateau. Heavy snow prompts migration to lower elevations in winter. The animals in summer may be observed in meadows along the Gibbon River, Elk Park, Madison Junction and the area between Madison Junction and West Entrance along the Madison River. Watch for them along the Firehole River and Nez Perce Creek in the Lower Geyser Basin. Wherever large meadows are located is a likely spot for observation.

Mule Deer

Mule Deer —*Odocoileus hemionus*

The Mule Deer is the only common deer species in the Park. The ears are large and mule-like. The tail is black tipped. The mature animals weigh from 140-200 pounds. In summer, the deer are yellowish brown but the coat changes to grayish in winter.

Mule Deer are scattered throughout the Park in broken woodlands and are commonly found along the edges of forests. In winter, they drift down to lower more protected ranges but not in migratory herds as is the case with elk.

Mule Deer are mostly browsers feeding on grass and sprouts, twigs, buds and leaves of trees and shrubs.

The high branched antlers produced on the bucks are shed every year during winter. When the antlers are growing, they are covered by a soft velvet-like skin which contains blood vessels bringing nourishment for the growing bone. The velvet is rubbed off on bushes and trees when the antlers are full grown.

Fawns are born in June and twins are not unusual. The fawns are spotted and the doe leaves them well hidden and untended while she feeds.

Bull Moose, Summer

Pronghorn

Pronghorn — *Antilocapra americana*

The Pronghorn is distinctly an American species. Pronghorns are unique in that the horns are branched and are produced on both male and female. The outer "sheath" is shed each year. They are the only hollow horned animals that shed their sheath.

Mature bucks weigh about 100 pounds and the does are slightly smaller. They are tawny colored with white underparts, a large white rump patch and white bands across the throat. The hairs of the rump patch can be erected to catch light and reflect it to flash warnings to other antelopes.

Pronghorns can run 60 miles an hour for short distances.

Twins are usually born to the does in June.

The Pronghorn are commonly observed in the Tower Fall area, in the Lamar Valley. They are frequently observed in the sagebrush flats near the North Entrance.

The food of these fleet animals consists of sagebrush, rabbitbrush, grasses and weeds.

Moose — *Alces alces*

The moose are the largest members of the deer family. A mature bull may weigh more than 1000 pounds. The Yellowstone moose are a sub-species called Shiras. Moose are the largest antlered mammals. The antlers are palmate and only the bulls produce them. The large heavy antlers are shed annually. Both bulls and cows have a bell which is a growth of skin and hair which hangs from the throat. Calves are born in the spring and remain with the cow for a year.

Moose browse on twigs and leaves. Willow is an important source of food. They also feed on water lilies and roots from submerged aquatics.

Moose are dark brown to black. They may be observed in marshy swampy areas such as at Pelican Creek, Lewis River, Madison River, Hayden Valley, Northeastern Road, East Entrance Road or in areas where willows and alders grow. Occasionally moose can be seen resting or feeding while partially submerged in water. Never underestimate the moose. Though sluggish in appearance, they are fast. A cow moose protecting its young can be a very dangerous animal.

Bison — *Bison bison*

The bison are frequently referred to as American buffalo. They are the largest North American land mammals. The bulls may weigh 2000 pounds. The cows are considerably smaller. Both bulls and cows have permanent true horns. The large head and large humped shoulders give credence to their massiveness. The calves are born in spring and look like the offspring of domestic cattle and are a reddish brown in color.

The Yellowstone Bison are one of the remnant groups of the former millions that once roamed the great plains. This large animal has a very uncertain disposition and should never be approached closely. They compete with the elk for food and frequent the warm thermal areas during winter. Though the larger herds go into the high country during the summer, they can occasionally be seen in open grasslands in the vicinity of major rivers. Summer visitors might see them in the Lower Geyser Basin meadows, Nez Perce Creek, Madison Junction, Pelican Creek meadows and Mary Mountain Trail to Canyon or Hayden Valley.

Bighorn Sheep Ram — *Ovis canadensis*

Both rams and ewes have horns. Those of the ram are large and curved. The ewes' horns are slightly curved, slender and much smaller. The hair is straight and not woolly. The summer color of the Bighorn is a tan brown but in winter is much lighter. They have a yellowish-white rump patch and white underparts.

Late autumn is the mating season. One or two lambs are born in late spring.

During the summer, the Bighorn is at home in the rugged mountainous country particularly in the vicinity of Mount Washburn. They are sure-footed and adapted to rocky areas. The bottom of the feet are concave enabling them to walk, run and jump on rocks without fear. In winter, they migrate to the lower elevations near Mount Everts. Here they must compete for the winter range with Elk and Deer. It is an unforgettable thrill to observe a ram Bighorn Sheep standing stock still in statuesque repose on a high rocky crag. The Bighorn threatens to become another of our vanishing species.

Bighorn Sheep Rams

Two Bull Elk

Bison Cow and Calf

Bighorn Sheep Rams

123

Cats

The Mountain Lion (cougar), lynx, and bobcat are listed in the Yellowstone checklist, but are seldom seen since they are secretive hunters. The mountain lion can weigh up to 150 pounds and is much larger than the lynx and bobcat who weigh about 20 pounds. The bobcat has short ear tufts and roams over areas from rocky mountains to open shrubby country. The lynx prefers dense coniferous forests where its chief food is the snowshoe hare.

Dogs

The coyote is a common member of the dog family found in many habitats throughout the Park. It has coarse, thick, grayish-brown fur. Coyotes play a valuable role in helping to control rodents and, on occasion, larger mammals who have become weak or sick. The coyote is an effective predator animal which also helps keep the herds of grazing animals strong.

The gray wolf (timber wolf) and the red fox are relatives of the coyote. The gray wolf is on the checklist, but other sources indicate that it is no longer found in the Park. Its status, at best, would be rare. The red fox is not common, but it has been seen in Blacktail Valley along the road from Tower Fall to Mammoth.

Rabbits

The rabbit family is represented by the cottontail found at low elevations such as at Mammoth and the North Entrance; snowshoe hare in coniferous forests; and the whitetail jackrabbit found at higher elevations in sagebrush and grasslands. The Pika (cony) is found at even higher elevations in rocky areas on talus slopes. Pika are about 7 inches long with small ears and no tail.

Rodents

The rodent group includes squirrels, mice, moles, chipmunks, ground squirrels, marmots, flying-squirrels, pocket gophers, muskrats, beavers, and porcupines. They all have gnawing teeth. They vary in size from jumping mice weighing one ounce to beavers weighing up to 70 pounds. The Yellowbelly marmot lives in burrows in rocky mountainsides. They are also called woodchucks or whistle pigs because their call is shrill and whistle-like. The marmots, ground squirrels, and chipmunks are true hibernators.

The Uinta Ground Squirrels are common in sagebrush areas and can be seen at Mammoth and Tower Fall.

The chipmunks have stripes on their sides and faces.

The red squirrel is more gray than red. They are very common in coniferous forests where they feed on seeds from cones. They make huge squirrel caches where the cones are stored.

Golden-mantled ground squirrels are larger than chipmunks and have stripes on their sides, but not on their faces.

Porcupines are quilled rodents and eat shrubs and the bark of pine trees.

Beavers are rodents adapted for aquatic life with webbed hind feet and a broad, flat tail. They build lodges with undersurface entrances and construct dams to hold and back up the water. Their favorite food is aspen bark.

Weasels

The general appearance of members of this family varies widely. They have one thing in common, though—musk glands developed at the base of the tail. If the tail is elevated or swished, the secretions can be sprayed as a defensive weapon. The odor of the secretions from the skunk and mink are pungent and offensive. The scent of some members such as the marten is a musky, not unpleasant odor, however.

Members include weasels, martens, skunks, badgers, wolverines, fishers, otters, and mink. All are carnivorous and have strong jaws with enlarged canine teeth. They are flesh eaters. Many of them play important roles by keeping certain rodents such as squirrels, gophers, mice, and rabbits under control to maintain a proper balance in nature.

Weasels, both the long and short-tailed species, are fierce hunters and cover a wide range habitat where mice and vole are their chief source of food.

The wolverine and fisher are seldom observed. The wolverine is considered rare in Yellowstone.

The marten is a dweller of the coniferous forests where it feeds on the red squirrel.

Mink live along water courses. Their partly webbed hind feet help them to swim swiftly in search of small fish. They also prey on small animals including birds.

The otter is a large member of the weasel family and may weigh 20 pounds or more. It possesses webbed hind feet and a thick round tail which enables it to swim powerfully to obtain fish which is its chief source of food.

The badger is a flat-bodied powerful animal with white face markings. It lives in sagebrush areas where it feeds on various rodents.

In Yellowstone, the skunk prefers lower elevations. It is a flesh eater, but also eats bird eggs.

Bison Herd in Winter

Bull Elk in Winter

Bald Eagle

Bull Elk in Summer

Shrews

Shrews are among the most primitive mammals. They resemble mice, but are not related to them. They are small, grayish mammals with long tails. The ears are almost invisible. They have long pointed snouts and pinpoint eyes. Shrews are the tiniest mammals in the world. They prey upon insects. The dwarf shrew, which occurs in Grand Teton National Park, weighs a tenth of an ounce! The shrews listed in Yellowstone are: masked shrew, vagrant shrew, dusky shrew, and water shrew. They are most commonly seen in grassy areas along streams at lower elevations.

Bats

The bats are the only mammals that have developed structures for flight. They have greatly lengthened finger bones covered by membranes. These structures probably evolved during the Eocene Age, and there has been little change in bats to modern times. Bats fly mostly at night when insects are abundant in the air. They spend days hanging in caves or hollow trees. They are nearly helpless on the ground because their hind limbs are poorly developed and their forelimbs are relatively long.

In order to locate and avoid objects in the dark, bats send out sounds, probably high pitched squeaks, which echo back to their very sensitive ears. The following bats are found in Yellowstone: little brown bat, long eared bat, silver haired bat, hoary bat, and western big eared bat.

Reptiles

Reptiles are cold blooded i.e., their body temperature changes with environmental changes. The high elevations, long cold winters and short summers are generally unfavorable. The Prairie Rattlesnake (*Crotalus viridis*) is the only poisonous snake in Yellowstone. It is listed as rare and is found in a very limited area near the north boundary along the Gardner River. Other reptiles, none of them abundant,are the following: Bull Snake (*Pituophis catenifer*), Rubber Boa (*Charina bottae*), Western Garter Snake (*Thamnophis elegans*) and the Sagebrush Lizard (*Sceloporus graciosus*).

Amphibians

The Amphibians are represented by the Tiger Salamander (*Ambystoma tigrinum*) which is common. The Western Chorus Frog (*Pseudacris triseriata*) is abundant in Yellowstone. The Western Spotted Frog (*Rana pretiosa*) is common. The Leopard Frog (*Rana pipiens*) is found in the Park but is uncommon. The Western Toad (*Bufo boreas*) is common and the only toad listed.

CHECK LIST — MAMMALS

masked shrew
vagrant shrew
dusky shrew
water shrew
little brown bat
long eared bat
silver haired bat
big brown bat
hoary bat
western big eared bat
cony or pika
white tail jack rabbit
snowshoe hare
cottontail
yellowbelly marmot
Uinta ground squirrel
golden mantled ground squirrel
least chipmunk
yellow pine chipmunk
Uinta chipmunk
chickaree, red squirrel
flying squirrel
pocket gopher
beaver
white footed mouse
bushytail woodrat
red back vole
lemming mouse
meadow mouse—*Microtus richardsoni*
    —*Microtus pennsylvanicus*
    —*Microtus montanus*
    —*Microtus longicaudus*

muskrat
jumping mouse
porcupine
coyote
wolf
red fox
black bear
grizzly bear
raccoon
marten
fisher
short-tailed weasel
long-tailed weasel
mink
wolverine
badger
skunk
otter
cougar or mountain lion
lynx
bobcat
wapiti or elk
mule deer
white-tailed deer
moose
pronghorn or antelope
bison or buffalo
bighorn sheep

Suggested locations and seasons for sighting certain animals

As a general statement, large mammals are readily seen in May before elk and bison begin to disappear into the high country.

Mammal/Season	Probable Locations
Cony or Pika, year round	Rockslides such as Silver Gate above Mammoth
Yellowbelly marmot, summer only	Old Faithful nature trail to Observation Point, Canyon area on far side of river
Uinta ground squirrel, summer only	Open grassy areas of sagebrush
Pocket gopher, summer only	Tower Falls
Beaver, summer	Many of the present population are bank dwellers; such areas as Grayling Creek on the Gallatin side, lower Shoshone Creek, small ponds in the Mammoth area.
Red fox, year round	Blacktail Valley, along the road from Tower to Mammoth
Grizzly bear, spring summer	Grazing in places such as Gibbon meadows April-May; may be seen in mid-summer on far side of Yellowstone River in Hayden Valley; back roads such as old Tower and Bunsen Peak; rarely seen from roads
Badger, summer	Sagebrush valleys of northern part of Park, sometimes seen along road to Tower
Otter, year round	Yellowstone River in Hayden Valley, shore of Yellowstone Lake, Gibbon and other rivers.
Cougar, year round	(Very seldom reported) seems to be Tower Area, sometimes Hayden Valley; Mammoth-Sepulcher-Electric Peak area
Elk or wapiti, winter	Drive to NE Entrance, early and late hours best; may be seen in numbers on Hellroaring slopes
Year around	Clearwater Springs—Roaring Mountain area
Summer, fall	Norris area
Spring, fall	Lower Geyser Basin meadows
Mule deer, winter, summer	Mammoth, road from Mammoth to Golden Gate Swan Lake Flat

Bison Bull

Moose, spring, year round	Lava Creek, Tower Jct., NE Entrance road, Willow Park, Hayden Valley, Pelican Creek (lower) and Fishing Bridge
Pronghorn, year round	Old road Mammoth to Gardiner, road from North Entrance to Reese Creek, flat by N. Entrance station
Bison, fall, winter, spring	Lamar Valley and Soda Butte, Firehole Geyser Basins, especially Firehole Lake and Fountain Freight roads
Summer	Lower Geyser Basin and Madison Junction
Bighorn Sheep	
Winter	Slopes of Mt. Everts above road to Gardiner from Mammoth
Summer	Mt. Washburn, Mt. Everts, Specimen Ridge, and Fossil Forest Trail

Buffalo Bulls

ESTIMATED ANIMAL POPULATION
FROM ANNUAL WILDLIFE REPORTS

Pronghorn 588
Black Bear 500-650
Grizzly Bear 200
Bighorn Sheep 300
Bison 3,000-3,200
Mule Deer 2,100
Elk

      Northern Yellowstone Herd 19,000
      Gallatin Herd 6,000
      Madison-Firehole 1,500
      Other 1,500
      Total 39,000
Moose . . . . no estimate

Golden Mantled Ground Squirrel

Other animals listed:

Badger	common locally
Beaver	rare
Bobcat	rare
Chipmunk	common generally
Cougar	infrequent
Coyote	abundant generally
Fox, Red	rare
Gopher, Pocket	abundant locally
Lynx	rare
Marmot	common locally
Marten	common locally
Mink	common locally
Muskrat	common locally
Otter, River	common locally
Pika	common locally
Porcupine	common generally
Rabbit, Cottontail	common locally
Rabbit, Jack	rare
Rabbit, Snowshoe	common generally
Rodents, Small	abundant generally
Squirrel, Ground	abundant locally
Squirrel, Tree	abundant generally
Weasel	common generally
Wolf	rare
Wolverine	infrequent

133

SOME YELLOWSTONE BIRDS

The many bird species in Yellowstone is possible because of the great variety of habitats scattered over two-and-a-quarter-million-acres. Because all wildlife — including birds — is protected, they can live here undisturbed and rear their young. Pelicans, trumpeter swans, geese, ducks, and many other water birds find the habitat suited to their way of life. Great predators like eagles, hawks, and owls find the food they need and help to control the balance in nature by capturing rabbits and many rodents. Huge birds like the Great Blue Heron and Sandhill Cranes may be seen here in their natural environment. Also, there are many song birds and insects for these smaller birds to eat. Bird size ranges from the White Pelican to the Calliope humming birds. The colorful Western Tanager is but one of many colorful birds. The strange and interesting water ouzels that walk under water at the bottom of streams can be seen in the mountain areas. For ornithologists and those who observe birds for pleasure and identification, a checklist of Yellowstone birds follows.

LOONS
*Common Loon
GREBES
 Horned Grebe
*Eared Grebe
 Red-necked Grebe
 Western Grebe
*Pied-billed Grebe
PELICANS
*American White Pelican
CORMORANTS
*Double-crested Cormorant
HERONS AND BITTERNS
*Great Blue Heron
 Snowy Egret
 Black-crowned Night Heron
 American Bittern
WATERFOWL
 Tundra Swan
*Trumpeter Swan
*Canada Goose
 Snow Goose

*Mallard
*Gadwall
*Northern Pintail
*Green-winged Teal

*Blue-winged Teal
*Cinnamon Teal
*American Wigeon
*Northern Shoveler
 Wood Duck
*Redhead
*Ring-necked Duck
 Canvasback
*Lesser Scaup
 Common Goldeneye
*Barrow's Goldeneye
*Bufflehead
*Harlequin Duck
*Ruddy Duck
 Hooded Merganser
*Common Merganser
 Red-breasted Merganser

VULTURES, HAWKS AND FALCONS
 Turkey Vulture
*Northern Goshawk

*Sharp-shinned Hawk
*Cooper's Hawk
*Red-tailed Hawk
*Swainson's Hawk
 Rough-legged Hawk
*Ferruginous Hawk
*Golden Eagle
*Bald Eagle
*Northern Harrier
*Osprey
*Prairie Falcon
*Peregrine Falcon
 Merlin
*American Kestrel
GALLINACEOUS BIRDS
*Blue Grouse
*Ruffed Grouse
 Gray Partridge

134

CRANES*
*Sandhill Crane
Whooping Crane
RAILS AND COOTS
*Sora
*American Coot
PLOVERS
*Killdeer
Semipalmated Plover
Mountain Plover
SHOREBIRDS
*Common Snipe
Long-billed Curlew
*Spotted Sandpiper
Solitary Sandpiper
*Willet
Greater Yellowlegs
Lesser Yellowlegs
Pectoral Sandpiper
Baird's Sandpiper
Least Sandpiper
Marbled Godwit
Sanderling
American Avocet
Short-billed Dowitcher
Long-billed Dowitcher
Semipalmated Sandpiper
Western Sandpiper
PHALAROPES
*Wilson's Phalarope
Northern Phalarope
GULLS AND TERNS
*California Gull
*Ring-billed Gull
Franklin's Gull
Bonaparte's Gull
*Common Tern
*Caspian Tern
Black Tern
Forster's Tern
DOVES
*Mourning Dove
*Rock Dove

OWLS
*Western Screech Owl
*Great Horned Owl
Northern Pygmy Owl
Burrowing Owl
*Great Gray Owl
Long-eared Owl
Short-eared Owl
Boreal Owl
*Northern Saw-whet Owl
NIGHTHAWK
*Common Nighthawk
SWIFTS AND HUMMINGBIRDS
*White-throated Swift
*Broad-tailed Hummingbird
*Rufous Hummingbird
*Calliope Hummingbird
KINGFISHERS
*Belted Kingfisher
WOODPECKERS
*Common Flicker
*Lewis' Woodpecker
*Red-naped Sapsucker
*Williamson's Sapsucker
*Hairy Woodpecker
*Downy Wookpecker
*Black-backed
   Woodpecker
*Three-toed
   Woodpecker
FLYCATCHERS
*Eastern Kingbird
*Western Kingbird
Say's Phoebe
*Willow Flycatcher
*Hammond's Flycatcher
*Dusky Flycatcher
Western Flycatcher
*Western Wood Pewee
*Olive-sided Flycatcher
LARKS
*Horned Lark

SWALLOWS
*Violet-green Swallow
*Tree Swallow
*Bank Swallow
*Northern Rough-winged Swallow
*Barn Swallow
*Cliff Swallow
CROWS, MAGPIES AND JAYS
*Gray Jay
*Steller's Jay
*Black-billed Magpie
*Common Raven
*American Crow
Pinon Jay
*Clark's Nutcracker
CHICKADEES
*Black-capped Chickadee
*Mountain Chickadee
NUTHATCHES
*White-breasted Nuthatch
*Red-breasted Nuthatch
CREEPERS
*Brown Creeper
DIPPERS
*American Dipper
WRENS
*House Wren
*Marsh Wren
*Rock Wren
THRASHERS
*Gray Catbird
* Sage Thrasher
THRUSHES
*American Robin
*Hermit Thrush
*Swainson's Thrush
Veery
*Mountain Bluebird
*Townsend's Solitaire
KINGLETS
*Golden-crowned Kinglet
*Ruby-crowned Kinglet

Western Tanager

PIPITS
*Water Pipit
WAXWINGS
Bohemian Waxwing
Cedar Waxwing
SHRIKES
Northern Shrike
STARLINGS
*European Starling
VIREOS
Solitary Vireo
Red-eyed Vireo
*Warbling Vireo
WARBLERS
*Orange-crowned Warbler
*Yellow Warbler
*Yellow-rumped Warbler
*Townsend's Warbler
*MacGillivray's Warbler
*Common Yellowthroat
*Wilson's Warbler
*American Redstart
WEAVER FINCHES
House Sparrow

BLACKBIRDS AND ORIOLES
Bobolink
*Western Meadowlark
*Yellow-headed Blackbird
*Red-winged Blackbird
*Northern Oriole
*Brewer's Blackbird
*Brown-headed Cowbird
TANAGERS
*Western Tanager
GROSBEAKS, SPARROWS AND FINCHES
Black-headed Grosbeak
*Lazuli Bunting
*Evening Grosbeak
*Cassin's Finch
*Pine Grosbeak
*Rosy Finch
Common Redpoll
*Pine Siskin
*American Goldfinch
Red Crossbill
White-winged Crossbill
*Green-tailed Towhee

*Rufous-sided Towhee
Lark Bunting
*Savannah Sparrow
*Vesper Sparrow
*Lark Sparrow
*Dark-eyed Junco
American Tree Sparrow
*Chipping Sparrow
*Brewer's Sparros
*White-crowned Sparrow
Harris' Sparrow
*Lincoln Sparrow
*Song Sparrow
McCown's Longspur
Lapland Longspur
Snow Bunting

*indicates nesting species

PRESENT TYPES OF VEGETATION

1. **Aquatic communities.** — These are found in the streams and lakes and are made up of plants that grow in flowing or standing water.

2. **Sagebrush deserts.** — The great central plateau of the Park varies in elevation between 7,000 and 8,500 feet, but some of the northern end extends somewhat below 6,000 feet. The sagebrush deserts are typical of the lower portions, 6,000 to 7,500 feet. Between Mammoth and the North Entrance two other typical desert plants, Greasewood (*Sarcobatus vermiculatus*) and Pricklypear (*Opuntia polyacantha*), are found with the sagebrush. The climate of the Park, however, is not a desert climate and these deserts are very slowly and gradually being replaced by forests.

3. **Alpine and subalpine meadows.** — Characterized by grasses, sedges, and many kinds of flowers. Timberline in the Park is at approximately 10,000 feet. The alpine meadows are those above timberline, while the subalpine meadows are those below timberline. The chief difference in appearance of the two is due to the dwarf condition of all alpine plants. Both display a riot of color throughout most of the Park season. The only place in the Park where most visitors ever get above timberline, however, is on Mount Washburn.

4. **Douglas-fir forest.** — This type of forest occurs below 7,000 feet and is very limited in the Park. It is best seen at Tower Falls.

5. **Lodgepole pine forest.** — This is the most extensive type of plant community in the Park, covering nearly three-fourths of its area, mostly between 7,000 and 8,500 feet altitude. Lodgepole pine trees often grow in very dense stands, but they are adapted to a shallow soil. Their roots are very superficial, so that they are not well anchored, and the forest floor is usually covered with fallen trees. For this reason the fire hazard in this type of forest is very great during a dry season. Although this is the most extensive type of vegetation in the Park, it is a temporary one so far as the development of the vegetation is concerned and will normally be replaced, sooner or later, by spruce and fir.

6. **Aspen forest.** — The aspen is the only common broad-leaved tree in the Park. Aspen forests are not extensive in area, but because of the white bark and bright green foliage which becomes brilliantly yellow in autumn they are conspicuous. This type of vegetation often succeeds a forest fire and may also develop in moist depressions or ravines.

7. **Spruce-fir forest.** — Engelmann spruce and alpine fir have already replaced the lodgepole pine in the more favorable situations, especially in the higher elevations, since this forest extends to timberline.

THE FORESTS

Eighty-five percent of Yellowstone's land area is forested. Conifers, cone bearing trees, constitute the major tree types. Lodgepole pine makes up eighty percent of all tree types and is the most common tree in the Park. The remaining twenty percent include conifers and a few deciduous trees.

Lodgepole Pine — *Pinus contorta*

It is readily identified for it is the only two needle pine in the Park. The two needles in a bundle are surrounded by a sheath at the base. It grows in dense stands extensively at elevations between 7,000-8,500 feet over the great plateau area.

Limber Pine — *Pinus flexilis*

It is a member of the white pine family characterized by having five needles in a bunch. The needles are 2-3 inches long. The cones are greenish and 3-6 inches long. It prefers lower elevations such as at Mammoth where it is common. It is not common elsewhere in the Park.

Whitebark Pine — *Pinus albicaulis*

Like the Limber Pine it is five needled. The cones are short and thick with a purplish color. It is the timberline tree and is not common below 7,000 feet. At timberline it is dwarfed and gnarled. Above 8,600 feet it forms pure stands.

Engelmann Spruce — *Picea engelmannii*

The needles are borne singly around the stems. The needles are four sided, pointed and sharp. The oval cones are about two inches long and pendent. It is the only spruce in the Park and prefers moist situations along lake shores and moist ravines. It tolerates shaded areas.

Alpine Fir — *Abies lasiocarpa*

The cones are not pendent but stand upright on the uppermost branches. The cones secrete a yellow resin which glistens in the sun giving the appearance of lighted candles on the tree. The cones do not drop but, when mature, disintegrate and the seeds drop to the ground. The central spike around which the cone developed remains upright on the twig. The needles are scattered on the stem and are soft, flat and blunt at the end. Alpine fir grows to timberline and extends down to 7,000 feet. The lower branches are held down by snow and reproduce by vegetative propagation to produce the familiar snow mats observed on the slopes of Mt. Washburn. The bark is relatively smooth and produces blisters containing resin.

Douglas Fir — *Pseudotsuga menzesii*

The needles are similar to those of alpine fir being flat and blunt. The cones are pendent. No other tree in the Park has the three-toothed bracts which protrude between the scales. Douglas fir are common in the Mammoth and Tower Falls area. They are relatively large trees and their trunk diameters are the largest in Yellowstone. Elsewhere in the United States, these trees are among the most valuable lumber species.

The Rocky Mountain Red Cedar — *Juniperus scopulorum*

This small tree is a juniper. The needles are scale-like and the cones are berry-like. Their color is blue-gray. They are often gnarled and stunted and grow at lower elevations and are most common at Mammoth Hot Springs.

Quaking Aspen — *Populus tremuloides*

This aspen is the most common deciduous tree in Yellowstone. It is found throughout much of the Park but grows best at lower elevations where moist conditions prevail. The flattened petiole causes the leaf to tremble in the slightest breeze. The bark is the favorite food of the beaver and the cut and felled trees are used for dam construction and winter food. Elk and deer, especially in winter when grazing is poor, eat the bark.

Forces which change the forests of Yellowstone are fire, strong winds, insects, parasite plants such as dwarf mistletoe, and various fungi. Natural fires have been part of Yellowstone's environment for thousands of years prior to the arrival of modern man. Large fires burned at average intervals of 20 to 25 years in the low grasslands, at intervals of perhaps a century or more in the vast lodgepole pine forests, and less frequently in the grass-lands at high elevations.

Fire was such an important part of Yellowstone environment that various communities of plants and animals *required* periodic burning to persist. Some plants, such as the lodgepole pine, reproduce far more abundantly after a fire because the heat opens seed-bearing cones. Sunlight then reaches the forest floor and a new generation grows vigorously. Certain birds, such as the bluebird, mammals, and insects thrive in recently burned areas. The entire life system in Yellowstone is keyed to the periodic stress of natural fires.

Natural fires will be allowed to burn in the Park. Each area is bounded by natural firebreaks of water or topography. If a large fire approaches the boundary, control measures will be taken. Man-caused fires will continue to be suppressed throughout the Park.

DECIDUOUS OR BROAD-LEAF TREES

I. Willow Family — *Salicaceae.*

Simple, alternate leaves. Fruit a small capsule. Many tiny, cottony seeds. Flowers in catkins. Stamens and pistils on different trees.

A. Trees mostly with rounded or ovate leaves, buds covered with several scales.

Genus Populus

1. Leaves with much flattened petioles. Leaves rounded, short pointed, entire or finely toothed.

Aspen
Populus tremuloides

2. Leaves with round or roundish petioles.

a. Leaves broadly ovate or roundish, whitish beneath.

Balsam Poplar
Populus balsamifera

b. Leaves lanceolate to lance-ovate, green beneath.

(1) Leaves blunt or acute, 5-15 cm. long, 1-4 cm. wide.

Narrowleaf Cottonwood
Populus angustifolia

II. Birch Family — *Betulaceae*

Fruit a one seeded nut, sometimes with an involucre; flower monoecious in catkins; trees are shrubs with alternate often lobed, toothed leaves.

A. Fruits in spikes or catkins.

1. Bracts of the fruiting catkins papery, 3 lobed, falling with small nut.

Birch
Genus Betula

a. Bark dark brown or greenish brown; shrubs.

(1) Stems 5-20 feet high; leaves ovate, 3-6 cm. long; catkins 2-3 cm. long.

Red Birch
Betula fontinalis

(2) Stems, 1-8 feet high' leaves cuneate to obovate; 1-3 cm. long; catkins 1-2 cm. long.

Mt. Bog Birch
Betula glandulosa

2. Bracts of the fruiting catkin thick, not three lobed, persistent.

Genus Alnus

a. Trunks 10-30 feet high; leaves ovate-oblong, 2-4 in. long; catkins 8-12 mm. long.

Mountain Alder
Alnus tenuifolia

The aspen are the most common of the broad-leaf trees. Sargent Cottonwood (*Populus sargentii*) has been reported in Yellowstone.

The willows, members of the genus *Salix,* are common as shrubs along streams and marshy areas. There are several species.

BRIEF KEY FOR PINE FAMILY (Pinaceae)

A. Needles single, scattered; cones with papery scales.

1. Needles square or 4 angled, inserted on raised bases; cones pendent. Needles stiff and sharp.

Engelmann Spruce
Picea engelmannii

2. Needles flat.

a. Cones pendent, with three lobed bracts between scales.

Douglas Fir
Pseudotsuga menzesii

b. Cones erect in topmost branches of tree. Cones disintegrate when ripe, central spike remaining on branch. Cones purplish.

Alpine Fir
Abies lasiocarpa

B. Needles in clusters surrounded at base by a sheath.

1. Needles in cluster of two. Cones with woody scales.

Lodgepole Pine
Pinus contorta

2. Needles in cluster of five.
   a. Immature green cones 4-8 inches long, remaining intact at maturity.

   Limber Pine
   Pinus flexilis

   b. Immature purple cones 2-3 inches long, disindegrate at maturity.
   Whitebark Pine
   Pinus albicaulis

C. Needles awl-shaped or scale-like. Fruiting cones roundish and berry-like. Berry blue-gray.

Juniper
Juniperus scopulorum

COMMON SHRUBS

ASTER FAMILY

Sagebrush (*Artemisia*). A composite member of the Aster family. There are several species but *Artemisia tridentata* is most common. It is a grayish bush with a pungent odor found in many open areas. Its leaves were used as a 'tea' by mountain men for treatment of 'mountain fever' in the early days.

HEATH FAMILY

Labrador Tea (*Ledum*). White to pink flowers in terminal umbels. Evergreen and resinous shrubs. Leaves fragrant when crushed. Boggy Woods.

ROSE FAMILY

Spirea or Meadowsweet (*Spiraea*). Perfect white or pink flowers in terminal or axillary clusters.

Red Raspberry (*Rubus*). Aggregate fruit. A bramble type with stems woody and prickly. Edible fruit.

Thimbleberry (*Rubus*). Thimble shaped fruit, larger than raspberry. Open slopes along East Entrance Highway. Edible fruit.

Wild Rose (*Rosa*). Erect or climbing shrubs. Prickly stems. Flowers pink or red.

HONEYSUCKLE FAMILY

Twinpod (*Lonicera*). Flowers in pairs. Erect shrubs. Bracts of flower clusters large and leaf-like enclosing the fruit. Flowers pink. Leaves opposite, simple, entire.

142

Snowberry (*Symphoricarpus*). Flowers white or pink, united into a bell-shaped corolla. Flowers in axillary or terminal clusters. Leaves opposite, simple, entire.

SAXIFRAGE FAMILY

Wild Currant (*Ribes*). Bush-like. Stems prickly and often bristly. Flowers pink, white. Berry smooth. Host for white pine blister rust.

Wild Gooseberry (*Ribes*). Berry haired and acid. Stems prickly and often bristly. Flowers white, yellow. Host for white pine blister rust.

CORNACEAE FAMILY

Red Osier Dogwood (*Cornus*). Whorled leaves and white floral bracts. Red berried.

SALICACEAE

Willow (*Salix*). Leaves long and narrow. Buds with single scale. Leaves alternate, simple. Flowers appear before leaves in gray, greenish or yellow catkins with entire usually hairy scales.

PINE FAMILY

Ground Juniper (*Juniperus communis*). Fruiting cones roundish and berry-like. Evergreen shrubs. Blue berry-like fruit. Berry with pungent taste. Plant spreads mat-like.

SOME COMMON FLOWERS

Flowers, with their colorful blossoms, lend beauty and grace wherever they grow. In Yellowstone, their colors enrich the meadows, ponds, swamplands, mountains, forests, bogs, and even the geysers. (Remember that picking the wildflowers is strictly prohibited.)

Limited space permits the listing of relatively few of the many common flowers. If you are interested in the botanical classification, pamphlets and books are available in visitor centers and at stores in the Park.

Buttercup Family

Pasque Flower (*Pulsatilla*). Light purple flowers. Flowers cup shaped, then expanded. Stems and leaves hairy.

Virgin's Bower (*Clematis*). Along wooded trails.

Meadow Rue (*Thalictrum*). Leaves appear like maiden hair fern. Separate male and female plants.

Buttercup or Crowfoot (*Ranunculus*). Matted floating plants in rivers and streams and ponds. Flowers white and yellow.

Baneberry (*Actaea*). Shrub-like. White berries become brilliant red. Along trails in forested area.

Monkshood (*Aconitum*). Flower parts covered with hood-like helmet. Shaded forest areas.

Yellow Columbine (*Aquilegia*). Spurred petals. Leaves ternately compound.

Blue Larkspur (*Delphinium*). Five sepals, the back one spurred. Dwarf Larkspur found on geyser basins.

Oregon Grape (*Berberis*). Also called false holly. Leaves with spines.

Violet Family

Violets (*Viola*). Blue, white and yellow.

Mallow Family

Globemallow or Wild Hollyhock (*Iliamna*). Large bushlike plant with pink flowers. Along South and East Entrance highways.

Flax Family

Blue Flax or Wild Flax (*Linum*). Flowers flat or saucer-like.

Geranium Family

Wild Geranium (*Geranium*). Common throughout entire Park. Flowers blue, pink and white.

Pink Family

Chickweed or Mouse-eared Chickweed (*Cerastium*). Open areas. Petals with tiny cleft.

Purslane Family

Bitter-root (*Lewisia*). State flower of Montana.

Pyrola Family

Wintergreen or Pipsisewa (*Pyrola*). Forest areas.

Heath Family

Pinedrops (*Pterospora*). Stem red-brown. Tall. Flowers nodding in racemes. Plant feeds on humus. Saprophytic.

Bearberry or Kinnikinnic (*Arctostaphylus*). Low creeping shrub. Common in forests. Sometimes called Indian Tobacco.

Blueberry Family

Dwarf Huckleberry (*Vaccinium* or *Gaylussacia*). Shrub-like, Leather-like leaves. Edible berry.

Primrose Family

Shooting Star (*Dodecatheon*). Rose-purple. Sepals and petals reflexed to expose essential organs.

Evening Primrose Family

Fireweed (*Chamaenerium* or *Epilobium*). Very common. Tall. Flowers pink-purple. Conspicuous from mid-season on. Flowers arranged near top of stem.

Evening Primrose (*Onagra*). Flowers yellow.

Buckwheat Family

Bistort (*Polygonum*). Small white flowers. Meadows.

Umbrella Plant or Wild Buckwheat (*Eriogonum*). Flowers cream to white.

Sulphur Plant (*Eriogonum*). Flowers yellow.

Gentian Family

Rocky Mountain Blue Fringed Gentian (*Gentiana detonsa*). Deep blue almost violet color. Petals fringed. Declared official Yellowstone Park Flower February 21, 1958 by Supt. Lemuel A. Garrison.

Phlox Family

Ground Phlox (*Phlox*). Spreading mat-like plants along all highways. Flowers pink, blue and white.

Scarlet Gilia or Trumpet Flower (*Gilia*). Calyx tube shaped. Along South Entrance.

Waterleaf Family

Blue Phacelia (*Phacelia*). Leaves and stems hirsute.

Borage Family

Forget-Me-Not (*Myosotis*). Small blue flowers.

Chiming Bells (*Mertensia*). Flowers blue in cymes, panicles or racemes.

Figwort Family

Beardtongue or Pentstemon (*Pentstemon*). Flowers blue. Irregular two lipped corolla and resembles snapdragon flowers.

Yellow Monkey Flower (*Mimulus*). Borders many streams. One of first flowers observed in geyser basins where flowers grow on banks of hot water streams. Common.

Red Monkey Flower (*Mimulus*). Along mountain sides and streams.

Indian Paint Brush (*Castillea*). Very common in red, cream and yellow.

Elephant Head (*Pedicularis* or *Elephantella*). Calyx not inflated and upper lip a long and trunk-like beak. Swamp areas.

Lousewort (*Pedicularis*). Yellow flowers. Swamp area.

Butter and Eggs (*Linaria*). Yellow and orange flower. Noxious weed.

Madder Family

Bedstraw (*Galium*). Small white flowers. Angled stems. Opposite or whorled leaves.

Mint Family

Prunella or Self-heal (*Prunella*).

Mint (*Mentha*). Strong mint odor.

Rose Family

Wild Strawberry (*Fragaria*). Smaller but resembles domestic strawberry.

Cinquefoil (*Potentilla*). Yellow rose-like flowers. Common. Open areas.

Pink Plume or Prarie Smoke (*Geum*). Flowers rose to pink. Style plumy in fruit. Common in open meadows.

Pea Family

Lupine (*Lupinus*). Blue flowers become a pod. Meadows and open forests.

Vetch (*Vicia*). Flowers yellow or blue. Fruit a pod.

Stonecrop Family

Yellow and Red Stonecrop (*Sedum*). Thick succulent leaves. Common on geyser basins.

Parsley Family

Cow Parsnip (*Angelica*). Tall. Large leaved. Small white flowers. Moist areas.

Honeysuckle Family

Twin Flower (*Linnaea borealis*). Somewhat woody, creeping herb. Pink or purplish color. Flowers terminal in pairs.

Harebell Family

Bluebell (*Campanula*). Blue bell shaped flowers. Blue to deep blue. Common throughout Park.

Water Lily Family

Yellow Water Lily (*Nuphar*). Large yellow flowers. Ponds and small lakes such as Isa Lake. Also called Wokus.

Iris Family

Blue-eyed Grass (*Sisyrinchium*). Purple flowers. Leaves grass-like.

Lily Family

Death Camas (*Zygadenus*). Yellowish or greenish white flowers. Bog or swamp and along streams.

Glacier Lily (*Erythronium*). Early yellow spring lily. Follows receding snow. Sometimes called Dogtooth violet but is not a violet.

Wild Onion (*Allium*). Several colors — red, blue and cream. Moist areas. Onion smell.

Orchid Family

Swamp or Bog Orchid (*Habenaria*). Flowers white, fragrant and in spikes.

Calypso (*Calypso*). Stems and leaves green. Flowers solitary and terminal. Lip sac-like with a tuft of yellow hairs. Rose colored flowers.

Coralroot (*Corallorrhiza*). Stems reddish-brown or purplish, the leaves represented by sheathing scales. Saprophyte. Common in forests.

Aster Family (Composites)

These plants are characterized by having the small flowers borne in dense involucrate heads. There are many tiny flowers crowded on a common head resembling a single flower such as in daisy, sunflower or dandelion. Composites are considered the most highly developed families in the plant kingdom. They are very numerous in the Park and only a few need to be listed here:

False Dandelion (*Agoseris*).
Goldenrod (*Solidago*).
Daisy Fleaban (*Erigeron*).
Pussy Toes (*Antennaria*).
Pearly Everlasting (*Anaphalis*).
Balsam Root (*Balsamorrhiza*).
Yarrow (*Achillea*).
Arnica (*Arnica*).
Everts Thistle (*Cirsium*).
Bride's Bouquet or Pincushion (*Chaenactis*).
Ox-eye Daisy (*Chrysanthemum*). Noxious weed.

Carrot Family (Ammiaceae)

Poison Hemlock (also Water Hemlock) (*Comium* or *Cicuta*). Moist areas along streams. Finely cut leaves and small white flowers in umbels.

The rare plants include:

Sundew (*Drosera*). Bog and swamp inhabiting insectivorous herbs having viscid glands on the leaves. Tiny hairs on the leaves.
Moonwort Fern (*Botrychium*). Bog and swamp environment. Related to ancient tree ferns.

The exotic plants include:

Butter and eggs, Canada Thistle, dalmatian toadflex, houndstongue, ox-eye daisy, and spotted Knapweed.

Note: Poison Ivy (*Toxicodendron*) has been reported along the Gardner River north of Mammoth Hot Springs. The herbage is poisonous to touch. Poison Oak (*Toxicodendron*) does not occur in Yellowstone National Park. Both are members of the family *Anacardiaceae*.

INDEX

A

INDEX

INDEX

INDEX

INDEX

INDEX

INDEX

INDEX

INDEX

PHOTOGRAPHS

FRONT COVER PHOTOS

Grand Canyon of the Yellowstone, Old Faithful, Tower Fall, West Thumb on Yellowstone Lake,
North Entrance Archway, Indian Paintbrush

BACK COVER PHOTOS

Bison & Calf, Yellowstone River, Elk, Lower Falls & Grand Canyon of Yellowstone in Winter

For additional copies of
**HAMILTON'S GUIDE TO
YELLOWSTONE NATIONAL PARK,**
mail check to:

HAMILTON STORES, INC.
MAMMOTH GENERAL STORE
P.O. BOX 188
YELLOWSTONE NATIONAL PARK
WYOMING 82190

I would like to order_____copies at $5.50 each (this
includes postage and handling). Enclosed is my check in
the amount of $_____. Please mail this order to:

NAME_____
(PLEASE PRINT)

ADDRESS _____

_____
CITY   STATE   ZIP

CUT ALONG LINE